ALSO BY HAROLD S. KUSHNER

The Lord Is My Shepherd
Living a Life That Matters
How Good Do We Have to Be?
To Life!
Who Needs God
When All You've Ever Wanted Isn't Enough
When Bad Things Happen to Good People
When Children Ask About God
Commanded to Live

OVERCOMING
LIFE'S
DISAPPOINTMENTS

OVERCOMING LIFE'S DISAPPOINTMENTS

Harold S. Kushner

ALFRED A. KNOPF *New York* 2006

THIS IS A BORZOI BOOK
PUBLISHED BY ALFRED A. KNOPF

ISBN : 978-1-4000-4057-5

Manufactured in the United States of America

Dedicated to the memory of my teachers,

Rabbi Israel H. Levinthal

Rabbi Mordecai M. Kaplan

Rabbi Mordecai Waxman

"The words of the sages echo even from the grave."

CONTENTS

First Words   ix

1. The Man Who Dared to Dream   3

2. Who Are You Working For?   27

3. A Hard Road, Not a Smooth One   49

4. New Dreams for Old Ones   68

5. Keeping Promises   99

6. It's Not All About You   119

7. The Mistakes Good People Make   134

8. How to Write Yourself a Happy Ending   154

FIRST WORDS

I**T IS** an intimidating thing to write a book in which Moses is the hero, considering that someone (Someone?) has already done that, and done it better than I could ever hope to. The only thing that gives me the courage to do it is that this is not really a book about Moses. It is a book about you and me, and what we can learn from the life of Moses, from his successes and from his disappointments. It is a tribute to the human quality of imagination, the ability to dream and to envision a better world than the one we live in, and to the human quality of resilience, the ability to go on bravely when those dreams don't come true. It is a book for all of us who have to deal with people who don't appreciate us, whether at home or at work, as Moses had to deal with an ungrateful people for forty years. It is a book for all the men and women who have begun to suspect that life will give them some of the things they yearn for but not everything, maybe not the things that mean the most to them.

I have dedicated this book to the memory of the three teachers who have shaped me to be the person, the writer that I am today:

Rabbi Israel Levinthal, the rabbi of my growing-up years in Brooklyn. He was a formidable preacher, often quoted, often borrowed from by other rabbis. It was from him that I learned to make the connection between biblical texts and people's concerns. To this day, whenever I sit down to write a sermon, I feel Rabbi Levinthal's presence hovering over my shoulder to make sure I take my preaching seriously.

Professor Mordecai Kaplan, Professor of the Philosophies of Religion at the Jewish Theological Seminary. The most original thinker the American Jewish community has produced, he was my mother's teacher in the 1920s and mine in the 1950s. Every line I have written in my ten books is in large measure a commentary on what Dr. Kaplan taught me in rabbinical school.

Rabbi Mordecai Waxman, senior rabbi at Temple Israel of Great Neck, Long Island. When I finished my military service, I served as his assistant for four years. It was there that I learned what it means to be a rabbi, when to meet people on their own terms, and when to challenge them to be more than they are.

I would like to think that their memories live on in my thoughts and that their teachings are given new life in my writings.

In this book, as in previous works, I have been blessed by the guidance and counsel of James H. Silberman and Jonathan Segal. Only they and I know how much better this book is because of their involvement. I am grateful, too, to my agent, Peter Ginsberg, for all he did before the first word of this book was written and for many months afterward. As always, my wife, Suzette, was a constant source of encouragement, especially during the sometimes difficult process of completing this work. If this book speaks to you and to your life, they deserve your thanks as well.

Overcoming
Life's
Disappointments

I

The Man
Who Dared to Dream

What happens to a dream deferred?
Does it dry up like a raisin in the sun?

Langston Hughes, "Harlem"

IN THESE lines, the poet Langston Hughes wonders what
happens to dreams that don't come true. I wonder what happens to the dreamer. How do people cope with the realization
that important dimensions of their lives will not turn out as
they hoped they would? A person's marriage isn't all he or she
anticipated. Someone doesn't get the promotion or the recognition he had set his heart on. Many of us look at the world and
see two groups of people, winners and losers: those who get
what they want out of life and those who don't. But in reality
life is more complicated than that. Nobody gets everything he
or she yearns for. I look at the world and see three sorts of people: those who dream boldly even as they realize that a lot of

3

their dreams will not come true; those who dream more mod-
estly and fear that even their modest dreams may not be realized; and those who are afraid to dream at all, lest they be
disappointed. I would wish for more people who dreamed
boldly and trusted their powers of resilience to see them
through the inevitable disappointments.

History is written by winners, so most history books are
about people who win. Most biographies, excluding works of
pure scholarship, are meant to inspire as much as to inform, so
they focus on a person's successes. But in real life, even the
most successful people see some of their efforts fail and even
the greatest of people learn to deal with failure, rejection, bereavement, and serious illness.

The lessons of this book will come in large part from examining the life of one of the most influential people who ever
lived, Moses, the hero of the Bible, the man who brought God's
word down to earth from the mountaintop. When we think of
Moses, we think of his triumphs: leading the Israelites out of
slavery, splitting the Red Sea, ascending Mount Sinai to receive
the tablets of the law. But Moses was a man who knew frustration and failure in his public and personal life at least as often
and as deeply as he knew fulfillment, and we, whose lives are
also a mix of fulfillment and disappointment, can learn from
his experiences. If he could overcome his monumental disappointments, we can learn to overcome ours.

What can we learn from Moses' story to help my congregant who is overlooked for a promotion or the elderly man or
woman whose children and grandchildren ignore him or her?
What can I learn from Moses to share with all the wives and
husbands who find it hard to feel affectionate toward a mate

who takes them for granted? Let us turn to the story of Moses, the man who dared to dream, to see what lessons it reveals.

Nobel Prize winner Elie Wiesel has written in *Messengers of God* that Moses was "the most solitary and the most powerful hero in biblical history . . . the man who changed the course of history by himself. After him, nothing was the same again." He goes on: "His passion for social justice, his struggle for national liberation, his triumphs and disappointments, his poetic inspiration, his gifts as a strategist and his organizational genius, his complex relationship with God and God's people . . . his efforts to reconcile the law with compassion, authority with integrity—no individual ever, anywhere accomplished so much for so many people in so many domains. His influence is boundless." The teachings of Jesus and Paul in the New Testament would be unintelligible unless read against the background of the Torah, the Five Books of Moses. The revelation to Muhammad at the inception of Islam assumes that the earlier revelation to Moses contained the authentic words of God. Even such secular prophets as Karl Marx and Sigmund Freud drew their passion for justice and freedom from the life and teachings of Moses.

We may think that we know about Moses, if not from Sunday school classes, then perhaps from one of the movies about his life. If we do, chances are that we relegate that knowledge to the dusty corner of our consciousness reserved for old Sunday school lessons, entertaining and probably edifying but not that relevant to our daily lives. But let me give you a fuller view of him, not only the man on the mountaintop, the man to whom God spoke with unparalleled intimacy, but Moses the human being, a man whose soaring triumphs were offset by crushing defeats in some of the things that mattered most to him, a man who came to realize the price his family paid for his successes. In the end, I trust we will still see him as a hero to admire and learn from, maybe even more heroic when the all-too-human qualities of longing, frustration, regret, and resiliency have been added to the portrait. Let me review his story, as told in the book of Exodus and the narrative portions of Leviticus, Numbers, and Deuteronomy.

Jacob, the third of the biblical patriarchs, son of Isaac and grandson of Abraham, moved his large family from Canaan to Egypt during one of the droughts that often afflicted that part of the world. There they were welcomed warmly in a country where Jacob's son Joseph, by a series of fortuitous events, had become an important government official and had arranged for Egypt to be the only country with abundant food during hard times. The clan of Israel (as Jacob was sometimes called) settled there and flourished.

A generation or two later, "there arose a new king in Egypt who knew not Joseph" (Exodus 1:8). The reference may be to a native Egyptian Pharaoh who resented the prominence of some of the non-Egyptians in his kingdom. He may have seen them as a threat to his rule and reduced them to slavery, setting them to the task of building the royal fortifications and storehouses.

Before long, the Pharaoh's contempt for the Hebrew slaves turned into irrational hatred. He commanded that all male Israelite babies be killed at birth, thrown into the Nile to drown (not a good way to maintain his slave labor force, but such is the power of irrational hate). The midwives who served the Hebrew population foiled his plan by sparing the babies and lying to Pharaoh, telling him that Israelite women were like animals, dropping their babies before the midwives could attend to them. Pharaoh believed their story because he needed to see the Israelites as less human than Egyptians in order to justify his treatment of them.

It was into this world that Moses was born. The narrative of his early years is typical of the hero narrative, the stories typically told about a child who will grow up to be someone special. The child is born to worthy parents, either after years of childlessness or at a time of great peril. He is separated from his parents and grows up ignorant of his heritage. We hear little of his early years, until he comes of age and is summoned to do great things.

To save the newborn child's life, Moses' mother places him in a basket, sets him afloat in the Nile, and sends his older sister, Miriam, to watch and see what happens to him. Pharaoh's daughter, having gone down to bathe in the Nile, finds him and adopts him. Why was Pharaoh's daughter bathing in the Nile when she had a houseful of servants available to draw her bath in the palace? One Talmudic sage suggests that she opposed her father's treatment of the Israelites (I picture her as an idealistic adolescent). She was going to immerse herself in the Nile to identify with the Hebrew slaves at the place of their greatest suffering and to cleanse herself of the shame of being Pharaoh's daughter.

Moses, having been adopted by Pharaoh, is raised in the palace, though the Bible tells of Pharaoh's daughter hiring Moses' own mother, whose breasts were still overflowing with milk, to be his nursemaid. In every other hero narrative I know of, from Oedipus to Harry Potter, the hero is born to noble parents and raised by peasants, with his real identity emerging years later. Only in the story of Moses is the hero born into a slave family and adopted by a king. The Bible would seem to imply that it is nobler to be a Hebrew slave than to be an Egyptian prince.

The Bible passes in silence over Moses' growing-up years. In one verse, he is an infant floating in the Nile. In the next (Exodus 2:11), he is a grown man. Again this is typical of the hero narrative. In the New Testament, three of the four gospels totally omit any reference to Jesus' childhood or youth, and the fourth, the Gospel according to Luke, devotes only a single paragraph (Luke 2:41–51) to anything Jesus did between his birth and his emergence as an adult.

Now Moses' career begins. He leaves the privileged sanctuary of Pharaoh's palace. "When Moses had grown up, he went out to his brethren and witnessed their labors. He saw an Egyptian man beating a Hebrew, one of his kinsmen" (Exodus 2:11). Did Moses know that he himself was a Hebrew, protected from the fate of the other Israelites because he was Pharaoh's adopted grandson? Or is it only the narrator of the story who knows that the Hebrew slaves are Moses' brethren? Did Moses think of himself as an Egyptian? Granted, as an infant he was nursed by his birth mother who may have conveyed to him a sense of his true identity. But he would not have been nursed for more than two or three years at most, probably not long enough for him to be told anything he would understand or remember. I would like to think that, when the Bible refers to Moses' "brethren" and his "kinsmen," it is speaking of his readiness to identify with the oppressed, the downtrodden, the marginalized members of society. Despite his privileged upbringing, when he sees a strong Egyptian beating a weak Hebrew, his instinct is to identify with the weak, a phenomenon we have often seen as men and women from comfortable backgrounds identify with the oppressed in their society rather than with the privileged.

Moses not only feels sympathy and kinship for the slave who is being beaten, he intervenes to help him, striking down the Egyptian, killing him and burying his body. Later in the Torah, Moses will proclaim the word of God, "Thou shalt not murder" (not "Thou shalt not kill" [Exodus 20:13]), but will also proclaim, "Thou shalt not stand idly by when your neighbor's blood is shed" (Leviticus 19:16). From the very first words describing Moses as an adult, we come to see him as a man who sides with the oppressed and who unhesitatingly takes action to correct an injustice.

The next day, Moses sees two Hebrews fighting, or more likely, one Hebrew man beating up a weaker, more vulnerable neighbor (the biblical text refers to one of the combatants as "the offender," the one who was doing wrong). Moses challenges the aggressor: "Why do you strike your fellow?" The man responds, "Who made you a ruler over us? Do you mean to kill me as you killed the Egyptian?" (Exodus 2:13–14). Moses realizes that his deed of the previous day is known and that he is a wanted man. He flees Egypt and escapes into the desert of Midian. There he comes to the rescue of the daughters of the Midianite high priest Jethro who are being harassed by shepherds. Jethro takes Moses into his home and gives him his daughter Zipporah as his wife.

The brief incident of the quarreling Hebrews sounds two themes that will continue to shape Moses' life. The first is the pattern of Moses being threatened by men and saved by women. Pharaoh seeks his death along with that of all the Israelite male babies; Pharaoh's daughter, aided by Moses' sister and mother, rescue him even as the midwives rescued other

Israelite babies. The Egyptian authorities seek to punish him for killing the taskmaster; Zipporah prevails on her father to bring him into their home and becomes his wife. There is even a bizarre incident, which baffles the best of scholars, in which *God* threatens to kill Moses (was it a nightmare? a sudden illness attributed to God?) and Zipporah saves him (Exodus 4:24–26).

These experiences leave their mark on Moses' way of understanding the world. They teach him the importance of a safe, protective home in the midst of a dangerous world. They prepare him for his encounter with a God who is both male and female, simultaneously powerful and dangerous but also life-saving and protective. The God of Moses will sometimes show masculine-aggressive traits, raining down plagues on Egypt, striking down sinners by the hundreds and thousands, calling for the demolition of sites of idolatry. But that same God, though the Bible will refer to Him grammatically as male, will just as often display a feminine, nurturing side, bringing forth life, feeding the hungry, comforting the fearful, tending to the sick. Moses will come to recognize his own masculine and feminine sides, both the angry, destructive impulses welling up from within him (smiting the Egyptian and later quashing rebellions against his authority) and the tender, nurturing impulses (leading a people through a wilderness, providing them with food and water, both of which he will go on to do) as manifestations of God and of his own reach toward godliness.

The second theme sounded by that incident of the quarreling Hebrews will be an even more constant refrain in Moses' life. If, as the Bible emphasizes, there were no witnesses to his striking down the Egyptian except for the Hebrew man being beaten, how did the fact become known barely a day later? One commentator suggests that the Hebrew who challenged Moses on the second day was the same man he had saved from a beating the day before! Who else would have been in a position to know about it? Isn't it psychologically understandable that a man who had just been beaten up might himself look for someone weaker to beat up, in order to restore his sense of power? Moses has just learned his first lesson, to be repeated often in the ensuing years, about the ingratitude of people he has set out to help.

The cynical wisdom that "no good deed goes unpunished" may be true. Many people resent having favors done for them. Being in need of someone's help can make a person feel weak, less than competent. During the forty years that Moses will spend leading his people through the wilderness, there will be frequent occasions when they will forget that he was the one who brought them out of slavery. They will even forget how miserable slavery was. All they will know will be the discomfort of living in a wilderness, the uncertainty of finding food and water, the elusiveness of their destination, and the abundance of rules designed to keep them from doing what they might want to do. Moses' gifts of leadership through much of that time will be not only the heroism of the leader who struck off slavery's chains and parted the Red Sea, but the perseverance and loyalty of the leader who remains committed to his goals even when the people for whom he is working fail to appreciate him.

Joseph Campbell, the authority on mythology well known for his books and his appearances on public television with Bill Moyers, finds a pattern in the life of virtually every hero, historical or mythological. He describes a cycle of separation, initiation, and return. Confronting a society in turmoil, a person who has lived an ordinary life to that point leaves that society and spends years in exile or isolation. There he undergoes a transformative experience. He is exposed to a truth of which he had not previously been aware. He may be given a secret weapon, a charm, or a valuable bit of information that will enable him to carry out his task. He then returns home, as Campbell says in *The Hero with a Thousand Faces,* "armed with the power to bestow boons on his fellow man." Historian Arnold Toynbee uses the terms *detachment* and *transfiguration* to describe the same process. That is precisely what will happen to Moses following his flight from Egypt after killing the Egyptian.

I should emphasize that just because this pattern is a constant element of mythological tales doesn't mean that it is not true and did not really happen to Moses, or that his story was altered to fit the mythological hero pattern. Consider the life story of Martin Luther King Jr., so recent a figure that mythical elements have not yet crept into his story. Born into the segregated South, he left to study theology at Boston University, where he wrote his doctoral dissertation on the theology of nonviolence. He then returned to the South, armed with the knowledge, inspiration, and confidence to lead his people to freedom. His life story follows the mythological hero pattern to the letter, but it is in fact exactly what happened and thus can teach us to recognize that there may be historical as well as psychological truths in the myth-tales.

For that matter, we can see the young Franklin Roosevelt as a charming but lightweight political dilettante who had to withdraw from public life when he lost the use of his legs to polio.

The Man Who Dared to Dream

In those years of exile, he developed the strength of character that enabled him to become the leader he would go on to be.

To return to the biblical account: Moses then spends several years in the home of Jethro, long enough to father two sons. The Bible gives us no clue as to whether at this point in his life he knows he was born an Israelite or whether he thinks of himself as an Egyptian. When Zipporah brings him home for the first time and tells her father of how he had helped them, she says, "An Egyptian man rescued us from the shepherds" (Exodus 2:19). But now something happens that will change his life, and ultimately change the history of the world.

Moses is caring for Jethro's flock of sheep, pasturing them in the vicinity of a mountain considered holy by the Midianites, when he sees a bush that is on fire but does not burn up. Intrigued by the phenomenon, he approaches it, at which point God speaks to him out of the burning bush. (Many religions, from Judaism to Zoroastrianism, use light and fire as symbols for the presence of God, perhaps because light, like God, cannot be seen but permits us to see everything there is, perhaps because fire liberates the energy hidden in a log of wood or a lump of coal just as God liberates the potential energy to do good things that is hidden in every human being, just as God will be the fire that burns within Moses, enabling him to do the great things he will go on to do, but not consuming him in the process.) The voice from the bush identifies itself as "the God of your father, the God of your ancestors Abraham, Isaac, and Jacob," and says, "I have seen the suffering of My people in Egypt and am about to deliver them."

As I read the story, this may be the first time that Moses is told that he, like his forebears, is an Israelite, and although it may be too much to expect him to banish all oppression and

13

evil from the world and too little to deal with it one victim at a time, he can strike a blow for freedom and against cruelty by working for the freedom of his own people.

Moses' first instinct, understandably enough, is to plead inadequacy: "Who am I that I should go to Pharaoh and free the Israelites from Egypt?" (Exodus 3:11). With these words, Moses establishes the model of the Reluctant Prophet who, summoned by God to do daunting things, responds by recognizing the magnitude of the challenge and his own human limitations. Later Israelites called by God to the prophetic role will follow his example. Hardly anyone (Isaiah may be the only exception) relishes the challenge of being God's prophet, telling people things they do not like being told. In God's first charge to Moses' successor, Joshua, God has to tell him five times in eight sentences to be strong and not be intimidated (Joshua 1:2–9). The warrior Gideon pleads with God: "How can I deliver Israel? My clan is the humblest in the tribe of Menasseh and I am the youngest in my father's household" (Judges 6:15). Jeremiah responds to God's summons by pleading, "Oh Lord God, I don't know how to speak for I am still a boy" (Jeremiah 1:6). And Jonah famously tries to flee from God's presence instead of bringing God's word to the people of Nineveh, boarding a ship going in the opposite direction. It is a daunting, thankless job to bring God's word to people who don't want to hear it. Moses, knowing Pharaoh all too well, is terrified at the prospect of doing what God is asking of him.

To overcome Moses' understandable reluctance, God answers him in a sentence that is often overlooked but that I consider to be one of the most important verses in all of Scripture. When Moses says, "Who am I that I should go to Pharaoh?" God answers not by telling Moses who he is, but by telling him who

God is, saying, "I will be with you" (Exodus 3:12). When Moses, in the next verse, asks God, "What is Your name?" that is, what is Your nature? What kind of God are you? God replies, *"Ehyeh asher ehyeh,"* three words so vague as to be virtually untranslatable, usually rendered somewhat mystifyingly as "I am who I am" or "I will be what I will be." But the Hebrew word *ehyeh* is the same word God used just two verses earlier, "I will be with you."

As I understand it, that is God's name. That is what God is all about. God is the One who is with us when we have to do something we don't think we are capable of doing. God is the light shining in the midst of darkness, not to deny that there is darkness in the world but to reassure us that we do not have to be afraid of the darkness because darkness will always yield to light. As theologian David Griffin puts it in *God, Power, and Evil,* God is all-powerful, but God's power is not the power to control events; it is the power to enable people to deal with events beyond their, or even God's, power to control. I imagine God saying to Moses, Where do you think the impulse came from to strike down the Egyptian slavedriver, to intervene on the side of the powerless, to protect Jethro's daughters from the shepherds who harassed them? And who gave you the strength to do those things? It was because I was with you.

God is with the person who speaks out against injustice and exploitation. God is with the man or woman paralyzed by illness or accident who strives to lead a fulfilling life, and is with that person's family as they care for him or her. God is with the person who doubts his or her ability to resist the lure of alcohol, drugs, or extramarital sex. Perhaps the most comforting line in the entire Bible, if not in all of literature, is the verse from the Twenty-third Psalm, "Though I walk through the valley of the shadow of death, I will fear no evil *for Thou art with me*" (my italics). To the people who insist, What do you want of me? I'm only human, God promises to be with them, assuring them that with God at their side they can be more than "only human."

Moses returns to Egypt, and if his first attempt to intervene on behalf of the Israelites, breaking up a fight between two people, was met with resentment, his second and more ambitious effort fares no better. Pharaoh is predictably scornful of his demand ("Who is the Lord that I should heed Him?" [Exodus 5:2]), and the Israelites complain that his interference is only making things worse for them ("May God punish you for giving Pharaoh reasons to hate us and kill us" [Exodus 5:21]). But Moses perseveres. The Bible (Exodus 4:1–3, 7:8–10) describes God giving Moses the power to turn his walking stick into a snake, to impress the Israelites and to intimidate Pharaoh and his advisers. Why a snake? Is it only sleight of hand, a magic trick? One psychologist writing a study of Moses speculates that the snake, which sheds its skin so that it can grow, represents the ability of living creatures to change and transform themselves. Moses might be using the snake to say to the Israelites, You don't have to be slaves all your lives. Life offers other possibilities. You can lose your chains even as the snake sheds its skin. He performs the trick before Pharaoh as a way of saying, You don't have to continue being the harsh, cruel ruler you have been until now. Like the snake, you can grow and shed that identity. But the Israelites can't bring themselves to believe him and Pharaoh dismisses him.

God then rains a series of plagues upon the Egyptians—frogs, vermin, hail, locusts, three days of darkness. (The darkness could not have been caused by a solar eclipse, which lasts for minutes, not days. Perhaps a sandstorm blocked the sun, but then couldn't the Egyptians simply have lit candles to banish the darkness? I have long suspected that this plague was more a psychological than a meteorological darkness, that the Egyptians were emotionally battered by plague after plague and maybe even by having to confront their guilt about living comfortably in a society based on the exploitation of an oppressed minority. The Bible's description of the plague of darkness, that people could not see anyone else or move out of their seats [Exodus 10:23], sounds a lot like depression to me.)

And finally, when none of these plagues could persuade Pharaoh to let his slaves go free, Egypt is hit by the most terrible plague of all. As punishment for a society that killed Israelite children, a mysterious illness kills the firstborn child in every Egyptian home. At this point, Pharaoh relents and lets the people go.

Moses leads the Israelites out in triumph through the divided waters of the Red Sea, and brings them to the mountain, Mount Sinai, where God had first spoken to him from the burning bush. There one of the defining moments of human history takes place. In the midst of thunder and lightning and billowing smoke, the people hear God Himself proclaim the Ten Commandments as the basis of a covenant between a people and its God.

A covenant is like a contract, but more solemn and serious. More than an agreement, it is a binding commitment. Buying a house or a car involves a contract; once the deal is completed, the relationship between buyer and seller ends. Getting married is (or should be) a covenant, a lifelong, enduring obligation. In the covenant at Mount Sinai, the people of Israel agree to live a distinctive life, striving to bring holiness into every aspect of their lives: their diet, their dress, their speech, their treatment of the poor, the widow, the stranger. In everything they do, they will be mindful of the fact that they are living and acting in the presence of God. And God for His part promises to give them a land of their own, a proper showcase for their distinctive lifestyle.

The revelation at Mount Sinai came in two parts. First, the Ten Commandments were proclaimed publicly, in the hearing of all the people. Then Moses went up the mountain to be alone with God as God revealed to him several hundred additional laws by which He expected the Israelites to live.

What was the significance of the Ten Commandments, given the fact that earlier societies also deemed it wrong to murder, steal, lie under oath, or commit adultery? Two things make the revelation at Sinai distinctive and unprecedented. First, the opening words, "I am the Lord your God who brought you out of the land of Egypt, the house of bondage," established that these injunctions were not just a matter of practicality (what kind of world would it be if people were free to kill and steal?) but are the will of a God who had already introduced Himself into the lives of this particular people, demonstrating His concern for them by freeing them from oppression, and who was giving them these laws not to restrict their freedom (He reminds us that He is a God who stands for freedom) but out of love and concern for the content of their lives.

The serpent who said to Eve in the Garden of Eden, "Has not God said to you, You shall not eat of any tree in the garden?" (Genesis 3:1) was the first in the long line of spokespersons who would portray God as primarily interested in denying people their pleasures. Since then, many voices have followed the snake in posing a conflict between the allegedly "life-affirming" drive for pleasure, for food, wine, and sexual gratification without limits, and the "life-denying" killjoy voice of religion. Many people mistakenly include Sigmund Freud among those who advocate pursuing mental health by indulging, rather than repressing, our every instinct. (Freud would have been appalled at the thought.) In the Beatles movie *Yellow Submarine,* the villains are the Blue Meanies who are colored a dull, monochromatic blue and say No to every pleasure, in contrast to the brightly colored heroes who are unfettered by any inhibition. I know many Jews who see Judaism as nothing more than a lot of rules telling them what not to eat, when not to work, and whom not to marry, and at least as many Christians who see Christian morality as essentially condemning all sorts of normal behavior as sinful. That may be why God, before He utters a single commandment, identifies Himself as a liberator, telling the people, I am not forbidding murder, theft, and adultery in order to restrict your behavior and deny you pleasure. You may have left Egypt, but you will never really be free until you learn to control your anger, your lust, and your greed. A man trying to stop smoking or drinking, a woman trying to lose weight, a married person embroiled in an extramarital affair would understand that message.

Second, other societies that outlawed murder, theft, and adultery did it on a case-law basis: If someone kills another person, the following is his punishment. If he kills a slave, this is his punishment. If he damages someone's property, this is his punishment. The Ten Commandments introduce a word and a concept that have not been found in any earlier law code. That word is *Don't.* There will be case-law passages later in Scripture telling the authorities how to deal with murder, theft, adultery, and perjury when they occur. But the message of the Ten Commandments goes beyond saying that those things are illegal and will be punished. It proclaims that they are wrong. Not "If you do . . ." but "Thou shalt not!" It tells us that there are moral laws built into the universe just as there are physical laws. People who disregard the Ten Commandments will cause themselves harm even as people who disregard the laws of gravity or a healthful lifestyle will.

The innovative concept of the Ten Commandments is the vision of the perfectibility of human nature. Codes of law by definition deal with misbehavior, with violations. No society passes a law that reads, "If a person tells the truth in court . . . ," or "If someone respects his neighbor's property . . ." Law codes, including those found in the Bible, anticipate that human beings will do things they should not do. But God, in the language of the Ten Commandments, proclaims that human misbehavior is not inevitable. God does not demand the impossible of us. He does not command people to go for more than a day without food and water. He does not tell us to go back in time and undo the wrong things we have done. If God tells us to spend the rest of our lives without murdering, stealing, or cheating, it must be possible for people to do so.

The revelation at Sinai, the unprecedented fashioning of a covenant between a people and its God based not just on exclusive worship and offerings but on righteous behavior, should have been the crowning moment of Moses' life. But even here, Moses would discover that there are few moments of unalloyed happiness in a person's life. Life will always be lived with other people, and other people can be unreliable, unpredictable, and easily distracted.

After the revelation at Sinai, God summons Moses to spend

forty days and nights atop Mount Sinai, where God will reveal to him all the particulars of the law not contained in those
ten basic utterances, and will give him two tablets of stone
on which He had inscribed the Ten Commandments as the
essence of His covenant with Israel. Toward the end of those
forty days, the Israelites grow restless, concerned that something might have happened to Moses, that he might never
return. This infant nation, only a few months removed from
slavery, behaves much like a young child whose mother has
gone shopping and is late coming home. To ease their fears of
abandonment and perhaps to express their anger at Moses for
leaving them, like a child "getting even" with a neglectful parent by doing the one thing most likely to hurt the parent *(I'll
show you what happens if you're not here to take care of me),* they
prevail on Moses' brother, Aaron, to fashion a golden calf to
function, as perhaps Moses did, as a visible embodiment of
God's being with them. God is furious. Days after these people
had assented to the commandment not to worship idols and
not to make a graven image of God, they have done precisely
that. He sends Moses back down the mountain to see for himself how the people have betrayed Him. Moses is so distraught
at the sight of the Israelites dancing and celebrating around
the statue of the calf that he hurls the tablets of the law to the
ground, shattering them.

It may be that Moses broke the tablets out of anger; the
people had betrayed God as soon as Moses turned his back on
them. Perhaps he destroyed them out of frustration; the purpose of the Exodus was to set the people free so that they could
freely pledge themselves to God's service and this was how
they had misused that freedom! Perhaps he shattered the
tablets of the commandments out of a sense of futility; what

was the point of trying to teach people the will of God if they would not listen? When Freud studied Michelangelo's statue of Moses in Rome, he noticed that the tablets are *slipping* from Moses' grasp; he is not throwing them down in anger. In this interpretation, when Moses believed that he was bringing God's word to an eager people, no challenge was too much for him. When he came to believe that no one was heeding those words, it was more than he could do to bear them.

God summons Moses back to the mountaintop and together they forge a replacement set of the Ten Commandments. These are placed in a sacred receptacle sometimes called *aron ha-berit* (the Ark of the Covenant, a term familiar to moviegoers from the film *Raiders of the Lost Ark*) and sometimes called *aron ha-edut,* the Ark of Witness. Was it witness to the fact that Israel had pledged itself to live by the terms of the Covenant, or to the fact that God was still in their midst even after they had angered Him by violating its terms?

As for the pieces of those original tablets, the ones that broke either because of Moses' anger or because of his despair, an old Jewish joke speculates that the people rushed forward to claim souvenirs of the stones autographed by God. The rich and powerful pushed their way to the front and grabbed the most attractive fragments, the ones that read "Kill," "Steal," and "Commit adultery," while the poor and weak were left with the pieces that read "Thou shalt not."

But another Jewish tradition offers a scene that, to me, epitomizes the greatness of Moses at least as much as his standing up to Pharaoh or his splitting the Red Sea. It is relatively easy to do the right thing, the demanding thing, when all is going well, but the real measure of a person's character is his behavior when things are going badly. In a scene that may well serve as the central metaphor of this entire book, Moses is pictured as lovingly gathering up the fragments and placing them in the Ark alongside the intact replacement set.

His dream of forging a nation of former slaves into a people who would unhesitatingly follow God's laws has been shattered. But he holds on to the broken pieces of the dream, to remind himself of what he once dreamed of doing and to remind himself of the lessons he learned when he found out that his dream would not be realized. Moses trades in that dream for a less ambitious but more realistic one. Yet he wanted to remember that he once had another, more hopeful dream, a dream that was so much a part of his soul that he cannot and does not want to forget it. He wants to remember that he once dreamed of achieving something great, something that turned out to be beyond his grasp, but he does not want that memory to brand him in his own mind as a failure. Those shattered fragments of what he once yearned to accomplish will not be millstones weighing him down. They will be stepping-stones, forming the foundation of future success.

The journey from the confinement of Egypt to the fulfillment of reaching the Promised Land could have been completed in a matter of months. But the evolution of a people from the mind-set of slavery to being comfortable with the obligations and uncertainties of freedom would take much longer. The Israelites demonstrated, by their complaining and lack of confidence, that they were not ready for nationhood. No matter how many miracles God performed on their behalf, they continued to doubt whether God really cared for them. If He did, they asked themselves, why would He have led them into this barren wilderness? Like many people raised in conditions of deprivation, they could not believe that they deserved to be cherished. In fact, the repeated miracles may only have reinforced their sense of helplessness and lack of worth. They would have to wander in the wilderness for forty years until the generation that had been raised in slavery gave way to a generation born in freedom.

Toward the end of the forty years, something happens that will again test Moses' capacity for surmounting disappointment. The people are thirsty, unable to find water for themselves and their flocks. God tells Moses to command a certain rock to gush forth water. Moses, for whatever reason, strikes the rock with his wonder-working staff instead of simply speaking to it, and water gushes forth. God tells him that because he did not follow God's instructions, he will die in the wilderness and never enter the Promised Land (Numbers 20:2–12).

It seems so terribly unfair to Moses, who has served God so faithfully for so many years, to be punished so harshly for what seems like a trivial offense. Is God so petty, so much of a stickler for detail? I have always suspected that there is more to the story than Moses being punished for a minor mistake. I believe that, in that moment, Moses betrayed the fact that he would be the wrong leader for the next chapter of Israel's history, the battle to conquer Canaan and settle there. He was worn down after forty years of responsibility. It is at that point that God says to him: Moses, you have served Me well for all these years. You confronted Pharaoh in My name. You led the Israelites across the sea and brought them to Sinai to embrace My covenant. You guided them through a trackless wilderness. But your time is over. Next year, Israel will need a warrior-leader, not a prophet, and you will attain your well-earned rest.

The last chapters of the book of Deuteronomy show Moses

as an old man, invited by God to climb a mountain in the land of Moab, and from there to see the land God promised to Israel, the land he himself will never enter. He comes to the end of his life not bitter, not feeling cheated, but as strong in his faith and as full of energy as when he was younger and had so much to hope for. "His eyes were not dimmed nor his vigor abated" (Deuteronomy 34:7). Typical of the spiritual greatness of the man, his gaze is forward, to the future, imagining his people settled in the land and living peacefully and purposefully there, at a time when many in his situation would have turned their mind to the past. Had he chosen to look back on his life, what might his thoughts have been? Here was a man who had stared down a king, who had molded a horde of slaves into a nation and taught them a way of life that would shape a majority of the human race for thousands of years. Did he remember that, or did he remember mostly the disappointments, the frustrations, the price his family had to pay because of his public role and responsibility?

Moses' triumphs were spectacular, but his frustrations and disappointments must have been searing. How did he do what he did? What qualities of soul inspired him to achieve what he did? What depth of faith enabled him to cope with the disappointments? And more important, even if we cannot aspire to reshape the world as Moses did, what can we learn from his story so that we too can do meaningful things in our own lives? What can we learn to enable us to cope with the inevitable failures we encounter so that we too will be able to come through them with our vision unclouded and our faith intact? Will we, like Moses, be able to hear the commanding voice of God in the bleakest of surroundings, summoning us to be more than we ever thought we could be and promising to be with us as we try to do that? And will we, like Moses, have the devotion to pick up the broken pieces of our most cherished dreams and carry them with us as we face our future?

In the Hasidic world of Eastern Europe in the late eighteenth century, there lived a sage by the name of Rabbi Zusya of Anipol, who was loved by all who knew him for his piety and his humility. As he grew old and feeble and realized that death was near, he became agitated. His disciples said to him, "Master, you have lived such an exemplary life. Surely God will reward you for it. Why then do you tremble at the prospect of dying?" He answered them: "When I stand before God, should God say to me, Zusya, why weren't you another Moses? I will have an answer for Him. I will say to Him, Master of the universe, You did not grant me the greatness of soul that you granted Moses. Should He ask me, Zusya, why were you not another King Solomon? I will say to Him, Because You did not bless me with the wisdom to be another King Solomon. But alas, what will I say to Him if He asks me, Zusya, why were you not Zusya? Why were you not the person I gave you the ability to be?"

What if, without aspiring to be another Moses, we could be *like* Moses in our ability to overcome disappointment, frustration, and the denial of our dreams? What if we could learn from Moses how to respond to disappointment with faith in ourselves and in our future and to respond to heartbreak with wisdom instead of bitterness and depression? Can Moses teach us not how to be another Moses, but how to be ourselves, our best selves, even when life doesn't turn out as we hoped it would? The answer is Yes.

2

Who Are
You Working For?

WHEN I ponder the greatness of Moses, the first word that comes to mind is *perseverance,* perseverance in the face of frequent criticism, dedication born of keeping his mind constantly focused on the presence and the promise of the God who summoned him and assured him that He would be with him.

One of my favorite stories tells of the prominent rabbi who ran into a member of his congregation in the street one day and said to him, "I haven't seen you in synagogue the past few weeks. Is everything all right?" The man answered, "Everything is fine, but I've been worshipping at a small synagogue on the other side of town." The rabbi responded, "I'm really surprised to hear that. I know the rabbi of that congregation. He's a nice enough fellow, but he's not the scholar that I am. He's not the preacher that I am. He's not the communal leader that I am. What can you possibly get from leaving my synagogue to worship at his?" The congregant replied, "That's all very true, but he has other qualities. For example, he can read minds, and he's teaching me how to read minds. I'll show you. Think of something. Concentrate on it. I'll read your mind and tell you what you were thinking of." The rabbi concentrated for a few moments and the congregant ventured, "You're thinking of the verse from the Psalms, 'I have set the Lord before me at all times' " (Psalms 16:8). The rabbi exclaimed, "Ha, you're wrong! I wasn't thinking about that at all," to which the congregant responded, "Yes, I know you weren't, and that's why I don't worship with you anymore."

What special wisdom, what special strength did Moses possess that enabled him to be an effective leader of an unappreciative people? Part of Moses' genius, part of what made him the effective leader and inspiring human being that he was, permitting him to retain his enthusiasm and his sanity in spite of everything, was that he remembered for whom he was working. He set the presence of God before him at all times. He believed in God's promise to be with him, and that made a difference.

When I think of all the things that made Moses great, it is impressive to realize what Moses could do in a single day, like confronting Pharaoh or splitting the Red Sea to lead the Israelites across. I am equally impressed by what he could do over the course of several weeks: calling down ten plagues on the Egyptians, spending forty days on the mountaintop receiving God's word. But more than anything else, I am impressed by what he could do day after day for forty years, serving as the leader of a people who, more often than not, did not want to be led and complained about the life into which he had led them. They hated the conditions of their wandering. They were troubled by the uncertainty of what lay ahead for them and their children, never quite believing they were capable of conquering and settling the Promised Land. And beneath it all, I suspect, they resented all the laws that Moses had imposed on them, telling them what they could and could not do, what they had to share with their neighbors and what they had to give back to God.

As we recall, Moses' problem started on his second day of involvement with his people. On the first day, he intervened to save a Hebrew slave who was being beaten by an Egyptian taskmaster, striking and killing the Egyptian. A day later, he intervened to break up a fight between two Hebrews, only to be told by the instigator, "Do you mean to kill me as you killed the Egyptian?" As suggested in the previous chapter, it may be that the instigator was the same man Moses had intervened to help a day earlier; how else would the deed, done privately with no one else around, have become known overnight? And psychologically that makes sense. Psychologist Dr. Levi Meier, writing out of what must have been a painful professional experience, comments in *Moses, the Prince, the Prophet:* "It should not surprise us that those whom we help sometimes turn on us. We help them at a time when they are most vulnerable, needy or embarrassed." People have often come to me for counseling, sharing embarrassing secrets about themselves—drug use, embezzlement, extramarital affairs. In those instances, one would have expected them to be grateful to me for trying to help them, but I often got the feeling when we met subsequently that they were uncomfortable in my presence. It may be that they were embarrassed because they knew I shared a shameful secret about them and seeing me reminded them of that, and reminded them of something they didn't like about themselves. Perhaps they suspected that I thought less of them because I knew it. (I'm too aware of human frailty to have let that happen. If anything, I thought more of them for wanting to face up to what they had done and for trying to change.) Or it may be that it is hard for a lot of people, especially men, to ask for help and appreciate being helped. It makes them feel incompetent.

MOSES' career as a leader began with an act of helpfulness that was met with resentment rather than gratitude, and continued in that vein for the entire forty years of his leadership. He led the people from slavery to freedom; they complained that freedom was too demanding, too unpredictable. He fed them in the wilderness; they complained that the food was monotonous. At one point, they nostalgically recalled what they were fed as slaves: "We remember the fish we used to eat free in Egypt, the cucumbers, the melons, the leeks, the onions and garlic" (Numbers 11:5). What were they saying when they spoke of eating free? Did they mean only that the taskmasters provided them with meals as they worked and did not charge them for it? Or as one commentator suggests, did they mean "free of having to decide anything, having to make choices," even as prisoners often find themselves overwhelmed by choices when they emerge from years of confinement (or, for that matter, as everyday shoppers find themselves overwhelmed when presented with more than four or five alternatives)?

Where did Moses get the strength of soul to overcome these frustrations and continue to serve as a leader? The story is told of a rabbi who had had such a busy week that he never got around to visiting sick members of his congregation in the hospital. As a result, he had to cancel a planned Sunday afternoon family outing in order to make his hospital visits. After an hour, he left the hospital feeling that he had wasted his time. Two of the people he had come to see had been discharged the previous afternoon (and were probably angry at him for not having come to see them earlier). Two more were sleeping and he hesitated to wake them. Another had a roomful of visitors and saw the rabbi's presence as an intrusion. And the last patient he visited spent twenty minutes complaining about her aches and pains and previous afflictions and cited them as the reasons she could no longer believe in God or the value of prayer. The rabbi could not help thinking of all the ways he would rather have spent that hour. Walking back to the parking lot unhappy with the demands of his job and feeling resentful, he passed an office building with a security guard in front. The guard wished him a good afternoon, which prompted the rabbi to stop and say to him, "It's Sunday. The building is closed and empty. Why are you standing here?" The guard answered. "I'm hired to make sure nobody breaks in to steal or vandalize anything. But what are you doing here in a suit and tie on a Sunday afternoon? Who do you work for?"

The rabbi was about to tell the guard the name of his congregation when he paused, reached into his pocket for a business card, and said, "Here's my name and phone number. I'll pay you five dollars a week to call me every Monday morning and ask me that question: Remind me to ask myself, Who do I work for?"

Moses always remembered who he worked for. He was not working to earn the thanks of the Israelites. He was not looking for compliments or appreciation (though he might well have welcomed them). He was working for God, obeying

31

God's call to bring the people out of Egypt, teach them how God wanted them to live, and guide them to the Promised Land. God, not the ungrateful populace, would judge whether he was doing his job well, and that gave him the energy and the determination to keep at his mission. Moses was able to be a leader because he knew where he wanted to go, and people followed him because they sensed that he knew where he was going.

Moses' goal was not only to get the Israelites out of slavery, but also to forge them into a special kind of community, to teach them to use their newly won freedom to become a people dedicated to doing the will of God. He understood that while God was opposed to one person enslaving another, God also wanted there to be somewhere in His world a community leading a God-centered life as an example for all people. We remember Moses' challenge to Pharaoh as "Let my people go." But what he actually said to Pharaoh was "Thus says the Lord, Let My people go *that they may serve Me*" (Exodus 9:1 [my italics]).

Moses promulgated laws about society's obligation to care for its most vulnerable members (there are more commandments in the Torah about sustaining the poor, the widow, and the stranger than on any other subject), but he was also concerned about what kind of society Israel would be. He wanted to fashion a community in which there would be no insurmountable gap between the most successful and the least successful, a community in which no one would feel hopelessly left behind and no one would feel immune from his neighbor's pain. The well-off may not have appreciated being told that sharing their resources with the less fortunate was an obligation, not a matter of charity. But Moses understood that those laws were meant to benefit the donors as well as the recipients. The wealthy members of society, the top executives who today make up to one hundred times the annual salary of some of their employees and add to their own income by firing some of those employees, would be better off spending some of that income to reduce poverty and inequality rather than spending it on security systems and gated communities. Moses' concern was for the well-being of all Israelites, not only some.

In much the same way, Abraham Lincoln, America's Moses, always remembered that his goal was not limited to winning the Civil War, leading the North to victory over the South. He recognized that the Southerners were Americans as well, even as the slaves were, and that the postwar United States would have to accommodate all of them. Lincoln's ultimate goal was the reestablishment of the union of all states that comprised the United States of America. Because that goal was in the forefront of his thinking, he could extend an olive branch to those who had waged war against him. He could say in his Second Inaugural Address—a speech that a professor of mine once called "the only modern document that could be inserted in the book of Isaiah and not seem out of place"—"With malice toward none and charity toward all . . . let us bind up this nation's wounds."

The wife and mother who often feels that her family doesn't appreciate her for all that she does and wonders why she keeps working so hard to balance her job, meals, and the demands of parenting when society seems to value almost any other kind of work more than it values the maintaining of a home, needs to remember that when she works so hard to make her home an inviting place and to put nourishing meals on the table, she is not doing it for herself, or for her husband and children. She is doing it for that mythical entity we call a family, because sustaining a family is what gives meaning to her life and what sustains the lives of her husband and children as well. She is working to uphold her image of herself as someone who does not compromise on the things that matter most to her. The man who feels unappreciated at work needs to remind himself that he is not only working for his supervisor, for his employer, or even for his paycheck, indispensable as that may be. He is working to maintain his own sense of integrity as a person who does what is right, who gives a full day's effort every day he shows up for work. Something dangerously corrosive happens to a person's soul when he no longer takes his work seriously enough to give it his best.

There was a moment in Jim Alderson's life when he had to ask himself for whom he was working. Alderson was an accountant for Quorum Health Group/Hospital Corporation of America when he realized that his employer was cheating its customers and cheating the United States government. As he relates his story in the January 2004 issue of *The Rotarian*, his employers asked him to keep two separate sets of books, one to show to the Medicare auditors for reimbursement purposes, the other to be marked: "CONFIDENTIAL, do not discuss or release to Medicare auditors." Alderson refused to go along with the fraud and was fired. Suing the company for wrongful termination, he discovered that the corporation that fired him was doing the same thing at hundreds of hospitals. He filed a whistle-blower complaint with the appropriate governmental authorities. The case dragged through the courts for years, during which time Alderson found himself unemployed and unemployable before he was finally vindicated with a large financial settlement and an acknowledgment of the truth of his allegations. The companies had to pay out more than $1 billion in fines, penalties, and reimbursements.

What gave Jim Alderson the courage and determination to do what he did at great personal cost? He knew who he was working for. He was not working for the greedy, dishonest corporate executives who signed his paycheck. He was working for his injured and afflicted neighbors who entered hospitals on the assumption that their well-being would be the hospitals' chief concern. As an accountant, he was working as the watchdog for American taxpayers whose dollars were supposed to be spent on legitimate Medicare expenses. And he was working to maintain a sense of himself as an honest man.

Alderson writes: "There were many, many times when I had to ask myself: Why am I doing this? You don't always know why, but then you see your kids and you realize you may have lost your job, your career, most of your savings, everything you've worked for, but if you ever lose *their* respect, it's something that cannot be replaced. I knew that when it was over, no matter how it turned out, I wanted to be able to look my kids in the eye and tell them that truth and honesty really do matter."

I remember reading about a man who would visit his wife in a nursing home every day. The woman suffered from Alzheimer's disease and could not recognize him. People asked him, "Why do you keep on going when she doesn't even know who you are?" He would answer, "Because I know who I am."

I know many people who, like Moses, remain committed to their jobs and their families out of a deeply rooted sense of loyalty that does not have to be nourished by appreciation. When I speak to gatherings of caregivers—teachers, hospice workers, social workers, doctors, and nurses—I always try to save the last ten minutes of my remarks to deal with the problem of "caregiver burnout." It can be so draining to deal with emotionally needy people all day long. It is so much less demanding to deal with facts and numbers than to deal with people. Facts and numbers behave; they do what you tell them to do without complaining or demanding anything. I urge caregivers not to be afraid to care about the people they deal with, not to be afraid to open themselves emotionally to someone else's pain and need. A patient may not thank a nurse for what she does. Indeed, the sicker he is, the harder it may be for him to stop thinking about his discomfort and remember to be grateful. But that nurse needs to keep in mind that she is not just changing someone's dressing; she is changing someone's life for the better in a small but necessary way.

I would suggest that caregivers burn out not from hard work but from a sense of futility, the concern that all their hard work is not making a difference. A Jewish legend tells that after Moses received the original set of the Ten Commandments from God atop Mount Sinai, he began to climb down the mountain to deliver God's word to the people. Moses was an old man and it was hard for him to negotiate the climb, but he did it because he was inspired by what he was doing. Halfway down the mountain, when he saw the Israelites dancing around the Golden Calf, the writing disappeared from the tablets and suddenly they were just two large, heavy stones, too heavy for Moses to handle. At that moment, they fell from his grasp and broke. When he thought he was doing something that made a difference to people, he could bear any burden. When he lost that sense of achievement, he became too discouraged to keep on doing the hard things that were asked of him. God had to summon Moses back to the mountaintop to work with him on fabricating a second set of tablets and to restore his sense of purpose before he could continue his task.

The difference we make in other people's lives is not always visible, not always articulated to us, but it is real. I once told a gathering of teachers in Minnesota: "You will read a magazine article about someone who came from the most unpromising of circumstances—inner-city ghetto, crime and drugs all around, absent father—and he or she went on to become a success and a role model, an outstanding athlete, a doctor or nurse, an effective politician. The interviewer will ask, How did you do it? And the answer will always begin with the same four words: There was this teacher. . . ." Somewhere along the line, a teacher saw a spark of promise in a student, lent the student books, bought the student meals, gave him or her the message, You can make something of yourself. As I read those articles, I often wished the interviewer would ask a follow-up question: Did you ever go back and tell that teacher what her intervention meant to you? One message from a grateful student will sustain a teacher's commitment to her profession for years. It will remind her why she remains a teacher and assure her that, for every student who bothers to tell her "You changed my life," there may be dozens, even hundreds, who could say that.

Moses drew the strength that enabled him to persevere not from the gratitude and appreciation of the people he led, but from the God who led him, who had summoned him and promised to be with him, a God who, in the words of a later prophet, renews the strength of those who trust in Him so that they can walk and not grow weary (Isaiah 40:31).

Sometimes the wisdom we need in order to remain loyal to people who may not repay our loyalty is the wisdom to recognize, as Moses did, the frailty of the human soul. People are not perfect. People are often weak, selfish, unreliable, and easily distracted. But just as God would be lonely if He could love only people who remembered to thank Him, we would be lonely if we read people out of our lives for not appreciating what we do for them. A large part of Moses' wisdom was his ability to keep sight of the goodness in people, even in people who disappointed him deeply. He could look at the Israelites after the giving of the Law and see how many of God's rules they were breaking every day. But at the same time, he was able to see them doing good things—acts of kindness, acts of self-restraint, acts of charity—that they would not have done had they not come into the presence of God at Sinai. They were less than they might be, maybe even less than they should be, but they were more than they had once been, and that insight was enough to keep him going.

An astute commentator finds an important lesson in one of the most obscure verses in the Torah. Chapter 13 of the book of Leviticus tells the community how to deal with the case of a man who is quarantined after contracting a highly contagious skin disease. (Bible translations generally refer to it as leprosy, but it was not the serious ailment that we today know as leprosy. It was a transient but very contagious skin condition.) We read in Leviticus 13:3–4 that twice a week the kohen, the village priest who was also the medical authority, was to examine the person to see if the skin lesions were superficial or if they extended deep into the skin, and to evaluate whether the person was ready to be reintegrated into society. That prompts the commentator to remark that in order to estimate accurately the depth of the wound, both of the kohen's eyes would have to be functioning properly. He has to be able to see the infection but also the healthy flesh around it. He needs to be able to judge whether the affliction is superficial and easily healed or whether it is on its way to becoming a lasting part of the individual. As the commentator puts it, "A one-eyed priest cannot judge cases of impurity." He would see only the sore and not the whole person. To be a communal or religious leader, to be a healer, one must be able to see people with both eyes, to see their festering sores but also the parts of them that remain clean and healthy, to see their faults and weaknesses but simultaneously to see their strengths and resources for growth. To be a husband or wife, to be a parent, is inevitably to be aware of so many disappointing, exasperating things about your mate or child, but at the same time to see those people in depth, to see them with both eyes, and be reminded of why you still love them.

PERHAPS the most challenging thing we will ever be called on to do is to remain aware of the redeeming qualities of people who have hurt or disappointed us. The last third of the book of Genesis tells the story of Joseph and his brothers, and it teaches us that lesson in a powerful narrative of family dynamics. The patriarch Jacob, who as a child had known the pain of having his father favor his brother over him, repeats his father's mistake, doting more on his son Joseph than on any of his other children. The brothers' jealousy and hatred drive them to abduct Joseph and nearly kill him. Judah, not the eldest of the brothers but the one with the clearest leadership abilities (King David would come from the tribe of Judah and biblical tradition holds that the Messiah will as well), persuades them not to kill Joseph but to sell him as a slave to a passing caravan on its way to Egypt and then to tell their father that Joseph had been killed by a wild animal. By a series of fortuitous events, Joseph rises from his lowly station to a position of great responsibility by interpreting Pharaoh's dream to forecast seven years of plenty to be followed by seven years of famine. Forewarned, only Egypt has stored enough grain to feed its people and sell the surplus when the famine strikes. Joseph's brothers are among those who come to Egypt to buy food. He recognizes them but they do not recognize him. He devises an elaborate ruse, not to torment them but to test them and see whether they have changed over time. He imprisons Benjamin, his only full brother, the other son of Jacob's beloved wife Rachel, the child who has replaced him as his father's favorite, and tells the others that they are free to go as long as Benjamin remains in prison. Will they, because of their jealousy, once again betray the favored brother?

At this point, Judah steps forward as spokesman for the brothers. His words move Joseph to tears and lead him to reveal his identity. Judah speaks of their elderly father and how much he loves his youngest son, Benjamin, whose mother died giving birth to him. He speaks of the pain it would cause their elderly father if the child did not return, possibly causing his death from grief. He uses the word *father* fourteen times in sixteen verses (Genesis 44:19–34), speaking of his father's advanced age, the losses he has known, and his tenuous hold on life. What has transformed Judah from a son who wanted to sell his brother into slavery to a son who is desperate to avoid causing his father any more grief? The years, and some painful experiences along the way, have brought him a substantial measure of wisdom and compassion. Having himself felt the pain of the loss of a child (Genesis 38:6–10), he understands the pain his actions of twenty years earlier caused his father. He knows that his father still plays favorites. He knows that his father loves Benjamin more than he loves him or any of the other children. But that knowledge no longer provokes rage or the wish to hurt his father. Judah understands that he will never change his father. He only has power over his own actions and reactions. He has to choose between accepting and loving his father as he is, with all of his maddening faults, or estranging himself from his father at great emotional cost to them both. He chooses to forgive his father for his favoritism, for being a flawed, imperfect father. Judah is now capable of loving his father and putting his own needs second, in order to spare his father any further anguish. This is the Judah whom Jacob on his death bed will bless as the future leader of the clan (Genesis 49:8).

I find the story of Jacob and Judah a useful one to tell to my congregants who complain about overcontrolling parents and to those who complain about neglectful children. I would tell that story to husbands and wives who are contemplating divorce because their mates turned out to be less perfect than they once thought they were. I would tell it to my rabbinic colleague who is frustrated by his synagogue leadership, reminding him that they are volunteers, men and women who have limited time and limited insight; they are not villains but people simply trying to do the best they can for their community, even though they will often be misguided in their efforts. Sometimes our personal and professional relationships stimulate people to grow and become more than they were before. But sometimes those relationships require us to recognize people's limitations and accept them as they are. We can do our best to change people, to summon them to be whom they are capable of being, but ultimately the only people we will always have the power to change will be ourselves.

The greatest challenge to Moses' leadership and to his ability to remain dedicated to a people who did not always appreciate what he did for them came in the episode of the Golden Calf. As we have seen, days after accepting the obligations of the Ten Commandments, during Moses' prolonged time on the mountaintop to receive more commandments, the people fashioned an idol and danced around it, proclaiming, "This is the God who brought us up out of Egypt!" (Read chapter 32 of Exodus carefully and you begin to suspect that the Israelites, for all their complaining, knew how much Moses' leadership meant to them. It seems that they wanted the calf to replace the absent Moses as the visible embodiment of God's presence in their midst. Of course, Moses saw only the calf. He never heard the discussion, found in the biblical text, about how much they missed him. And, of course, they never took the time to tell him.) Moses was furious at the people's betrayal of the Covenant and let the tablets fall to the ground, shattering them.

Moses' dream of forging the former slaves into a people who would unhesitatingly follow God's laws has been shattered. But we recall that he holds on to the broken pieces of the dream, to remind himself of what he once dreamed of doing and to remind himself of the lessons he learned when he discovered that his dream would not be realized. And then he ascends the mountain once more, to fashion a second set of tablets that will bear the same words.

But there is a difference. The first set of tablets was fashioned by God. As for the second set, God instructs Moses,

"Carve for yourself two tablets of stone like the first, and I will inscribe upon them the words that were on the first tablets" (Exodus 34:1 [my italics]). The replacement tablets, unlike the originals, will be a joint human-divine effort. If the original tablets came from God and reflected the perfection of God, the second set reflected the will of God and the ideals of God filtered through the limitations of human beings and the reality of human experience. Moses (and perhaps even God) has learned a valuable lesson: we can and should set high standards for people, but at the same time we must be prepared to see them fall short of those high standards. For the rest of his life, Moses would keep the pieces of the original tablets in the Ark of the Covenant alongside the intact second set, to remind himself of that lesson.

Estelle Frankel, a gifted therapist who combines the wisdom of the Jewish mystical tradition with the insights of modern therapy, writes in her book *Sacred Therapy:*

> The two revelations at Sinai can also be seen as symbolizing the inevitable stages we go through in our spiritual development. The first tablets, like the initial visions we have for our lives, frequently shatter, especially when they are based on naïvely idealistic assumptions. . . . Our very conceptions of God and our assumptions about the meaning of faith may shatter as we bump up against the morally complex and often contradictory aspects of the real world. Yet if we learn from our mistakes and find ways to pick up the broken pieces of shattered dreams, we can go on to re-create our lives out of the rubble of our initial failures. And ultimately we become wiser and more complex as our youthful ideals are replaced by more realistic and sustainable ones. . . . The

myth of the broken tablets teaches us that when we abandon old pathways, it is important that we hold on to the beauty and essence of the dreams we once held dear . . . for ultimately the whole and the broken live side by side in us all.

Dr. Levi Meier, when he counsels religiously committed couples in a troubled relationship, often uses the story of the Golden Calf and the breaking of the tablets as a healing device. He writes in his book on Moses: "The sad truth is that in every relationship involving love and trust, there exist the seeds of betrayal. . . . Such betrayals can be repaired. However the new level of trust is different from what existed before. It is built upon the reality of experience rather than on innocent hopes and dreams."

What Dr. Meier calls betrayal, I would rather think of as "unreliability." The word *betrayal,* whether used by Moses about the Israelites and their statue or by a wife whose husband has been caught in an affair, sounds so drastic, so final. Traitors are shot; unreliable people are rehabilitated. I see the story of the Golden Calf, and of Moses holding on to the broken tablets alongside the new ones, as telling us that the Covenant has been broken but can be renewed. The covenantal relationship between God and His people has been damaged but not ended.

For Moses, the words on the first set of tablets, the ones carved by God, were demands that turned out to be too much for the people. The words on the second set, a joint effort of God and devoted humans, were a vision, a summons to be more than we are, and as such they endure to this day.

It has been said that "the world breaks everyone and afterward many are stronger at the broken places." My experience has been that that is often, but not always, true. Sometimes a broken leg leads to a permanent limp. But much of the time the fracture heals and the leg is actually stronger than it was before. Sometimes an act of irresponsibility, seen by one party as an unforgivable betrayal, breaks a relationship beyond repair. But I have found that much of the time, whether we are speaking of a marriage or just a friendship, the parties can forge a set of replacement tablets built "upon the reality of experience." There is a distinction, as one marriage counselor puts it, between "injuries to our soul," which cannot be repaired, and "injuries to our sensibilities," which may hurt but will heal. Sharon Salzberg, who writes on spiritual issues from a Buddhist perspective, has said in *Lovingkindness,* "When we open our hearts to pain and suffering, we begin to heal, not because suffering is redemptive but because opening our heart is."

When a wife whose husband has been unfaithful says to me, "I can't look at him without picturing in my mind what he was doing with her when I thought he was working late at the office to support our family," I would say to her, "I understand, and I'm certainly not going to make a case for the acceptability of adultery. Neither am I going to ask you to accept any of the blame for driving him into the arms of another woman. But when you look at him and think of that, what exactly are you seeing? Are you seeing a selfish, unfaithful liar? Or are you seeing a man who is good and strong in some ways but too weak to resist this particular temptation? If he is prepared to correct that weakness and not repeat it, are you capable of living in a marriage that has a large crack in it that has been plastered over? Can you look at your husband the way the biblical kohen would look at a man with leprosy, and see his healthy parts along with his loathsome defects? I know your marriage will never be the same, but that doesn't mean it has to be discarded. All marriages go through a period of disillusionment when we discover that our partner isn't as perfect as we persuaded ourselves he or she was. That's what happened when Moses gave up on the original Ten Commandments and broke the tablets. But you know, that replacement set of tablets, based on hope and forgiveness rather than on demands and unrealistic expectations, has done pretty well. It has lasted for more than three thousand years."

Often we do become "stronger at the broken places." Think of two married couples. One couple insists that they have never had a serious quarrel in all the years they have been married. They have never spoken a harsh word to each other. Each considers the other his or her best friend in the world. The other couple has lost count of the number of angry, screaming, ashtray-throwing fights they have had. Time and again, they have found themselves wondering if their relationship had a future. But every time they pondered the option of separation, they would peer into the abyss and step back from it. They would remember how much they had shared and realize how much they cared for each other. Which relationship would you think to be stronger, more able to survive an unanticipated downturn or sudden tragedy? I would have more confidence in the second couple, who have been taught by experience how strong the bond between them is.

Nobel Prize–winning author Gabriel García Márquez writes in his autobiography, *Living to Tell the Tale,* about his father's philandering and his mother's tolerance of it, including welcoming into her home the several children he had fathered with other women in the course of his affairs. One night, when Gabriel and his brother came home at three in the morning after spending the night in the company of women of questionable virtue, their mother, who had stayed up waiting for them, sighed in exasperation and said, "You are going to be just like your papa." She then went on to say, "God willing, you will be husbands as good as he is." She had abundant reasons to feel betrayed and angry, but she chose instead to focus on what her husband brought to her life and what they had shared together. Like the biblical kohen, she could look at him with both eyes. She knew she had a part of him that none of those other women would ever have.

What, then, was the wisdom of Moses that enabled him to carry on day after day, year after year, as leader of a people who exasperated him more often than they appreciated him? It was a recognition of the frailty of the human character, the occasional unreliability of even the best of people, and the sometimes unexpected goodness of even the worst of them. It was his understanding that if he could not control the behavior or the emotions of others, he could control his own response to them, giving them room to be themselves and still being able to love them, even when the self that they chose to be was not one he would have chosen for them. Sometimes, by loving them rather than judging them, he would inspire them to grow and change in the direction he hoped for. But even if they didn't change, he loved them just the same. Part of the wisdom of Moses was his ability to cherish the broken pieces of his idealistic dream while replacing them with an alternative vision tempered by experience and reality.

Moses was wise enough to know that people will often disappoint you, that they will be weak and unreliable, that they will forget to thank you, but you must love them anyway. You must do the right thing not for the applause or the reward but because it is the right thing to do, and you must never forget who and what you are really working for. Like the man who visited his Alzheimer's-afflicted wife daily, do things for people not because of who they are or what they do in return, but because of who *you* are.

3

A Hard Road,
Not a Smooth One

Ultimately the whole and the broken
live side by side in us all.

Estelle Frankel, *Sacred Therapy*

W HAT DOES a person do with all the dreams that don't
come true—dreams of emerging talents, dreams of
careers, dreams of wealth and recognition, dreams of marriage
and family? Some people are able to do what Moses did when
he lovingly gathered up the fragments of the original Ten
Commandments. They manage to hold on to the memories of
those dreams without being weighed down by them, without
letting their unfulfilled dreams define them as failures. They
can cherish the memories of a time when they let their imagi-
nations soar, when they could imagine a more exciting, more
gratifying life for themselves. Others let themselves be defined
not by their dreams but by their disappointments, perpetually

frustrated by what they yearned for and never attained. For them, the broken pieces of their dreams are millstones rather than stepping-stones.

What happens to the dreamers, all those people whose lives haven't turned out as they hoped and planned? What do you do when you are confronted with rejection or failure, when a door is closed in your face, a door through which you very much wanted to enter? How do you find the will to go on when you realize that the life you are living is not the one you had been looking forward to? How did Moses manage to go on as a leader after being told that he would never enter the Promised Land? How must a college senior respond after being told that he or she is not cut out for medical school?

Every disappointment, every rejection, every dream that doesn't come true leaves a wound in a person's soul. Major setbacks—divorce, bereavement, infertility, crippling illness, losing your job—leave permanent scars. Small disappointments—being passed over for a promotion, having a close friend suddenly be too busy to find time for you—leave smaller wounds, but wounds nonetheless. The question is not, Can I get through life without some failures and rejections? because you can't, and the more you aspire to in your life, the more you yearn for, the more scars you will accumulate along the way. The real question is, How will you respond to those disappointments? Will you respond with bitterness, envy, and self-doubt, or with resilience and wisdom?

There is so much to admire and be grateful for about the American way of life, including the freedom of thought and speech it guarantees, the possibilities of success it offers. There are still many societies in the world where the shoemaker's son is expected to grow up to be a shoemaker and the baker's son to be a baker. In America, we have seen the shoemaker's child become a doctor or a judge and the baker's son or daughter become a successful real estate developer. But there is a dark side to this America of endless possibilities. Too often it leads to an uncritical worship of success and undeserved scorn for those who fail. We are too quick to celebrate unworthy, ruthless people who do whatever it takes to succeed, and too ready to dismiss people who come up short at one particular thing as being failures. (Do you remember the billboard put up by an athletic shoe company at the Atlanta Olympic games: YOU DIDN'T WIN THE SILVER; YOU LOST THE GOLD?) And what of all those public servants whose years of accomplishment are eclipsed by one final electoral defeat, so that they go down in the history books as "losers"?

I have known too many people who saw one of their cherished dreams disappear, perhaps through little or no fault of their own—a marriage that failed because of the immaturity of one's mate, a business that went bankrupt because of the incompetence or dishonesty of a key employee or changing market conditions, an adolescent son or daughter who took up with the wrong friends and fell afoul of the law—and they let that single development, shattering as it may have been, define them: they thought they had failed and therefore saw themselves as failures. I have counseled any number of women who, when they learned that they had given birth to a child with serious birth defects, said something to me along the lines of, So many stupid, uneducated women have healthy babies, and I can't even do that right.

I have known too many people who lost the ability to dream after having had their hearts broken. I have known too many parents who discouraged their children from dreaming, from aspiring to too much, lest they be hurt when their dreams failed. And I am convinced they would have done better to let their children dare to dream and assure them that when their dreams failed, they would have the strength and the resiliency to go on with their lives despite the disappointment.

From the first time I heard Judy Collins sing "The Rose," I have been haunted by the line "It's the heart afraid of breaking that never learns to dance." It spoke to me of all the people whose lives have been derailed by one serious failure, people whose fondest hopes never worked out, and as a result they had lost the ability to hope, the courage to dream. Then one day in a souvenir shop in Venice, California, I found, of all things, a refrigerator magnet that gave me the answer to the song's lament. It read DANCE AS IF NO ONE WAS WATCHING; LOVE AS IF YOU'D NEVER BEEN HURT.

Where can you find the courage, the will to go on with your life carrying the broken shards of the dreams you started out with, even as Moses carried with him the fragments of the original Ten Commandments? It doesn't help to be told that life is not fair. It is of limited comfort to be assured that God cherishes the brokenhearted more than He does successful people because they have been purged of their arrogance and unrealistic expectations. (Think of the line from *Fiddler on the Roof* when Tevye is told that wealth is a curse and he responds, "May God smite me with it and may I never recover.") And no matter how comforting a vision of a life beyond this life may be, where the last shall be first and the brokenhearted made whole, it does not really solve the problem for people who still need to go on living in this world, where they feel condemned to finish last.

I hate to think that experience will teach us not to dream,

not to yearn for happiness or fulfillment. I want people to dare to dream, to be brave enough to dream even as they realize that many of our dreams won't come true. To dream is to imagine a world and a life better than the one we know now.

Perhaps failure and disappointment can teach us that we may fail at one thing, we may fail at several things, but that does not mean that we are failures as people. The worth of a person's soul is not measured by the size of his or her bank account or the volume of the applause a person evokes, but by one's humanity, by one's compassion, even by the courage to keep on dreaming amid the broken pieces of our earlier dreams. True success consists not in becoming the person you dreamed of being when you were young, but in becoming the person you were meant to be, the person you are capable of being when you are at your best. As I suggested earlier, the question is not "Zusya, why were you not Moses?" but rather "Why were you not Zusya?"

Perhaps the enduring lesson of our failures is the one I learned from reading one of the great books of the twentieth century, Viktor Frankl's *Man's Search for Meaning*. Frankl was a prominent psychiatrist living in Vienna when Nazi Germany absorbed Austria in March 1938. Because he was a Jew, he was interned in Auschwitz but was fortunate enough to survive. Looking back on his Auschwitz experience, he wrote, "Everything can be taken from a man but the last of human freedoms, the right to choose one's attitude in any given set of circumstances." In other words, *what happens to you, no matter how hurtful or unfair, is ultimately less important than what you do about what happens to you.*

Consider the athletically gifted teenager who sees basketball as his ticket out of poverty and the inner city. His skills make him an all-star in high school, and then a useful substitute on a major college team. But they are never enough for him to become a professional. How does he respond? Does he go back to the ghetto, rejected and hopeless, to hang around the school-yards and bore people with accounts of what might have been? (In the words of one ex-athlete, "The older I get, the better I used to be.") Or does he find another road out of the ghetto and pursue it with the same dedication he once brought to his basketball game?

I have counseled too many women over the years whose husbands had left them after a dozen or so years of marriage and promptly found a younger woman to marry. Some of those women became bitter, brittle, and unforgiving, unable to trust a man again, unable to believe in their own ability to sustain a relationship. Others, after a period of adjustment, discovered what it felt like to be a whole person in their own right rather than half of a couple, often saying something to me like, Can you believe how long I was miserable over not having that selfish, lying jerk in my life? I'm lucky to be rid of him. They chose to define themselves not by what had been done to them but by how they responded to it.

Richard Russo, in his novel *Empire Falls,* writes of a local high school hockey star, the pride of his town, who never made it as a professional. "What did you do when you were good at just one thing, after it turned out you weren't as good as you thought?" Elsewhere Russo's narrator, contemplating a couple who had started out with idealistic dreams only to settle for a less fulfilling but highly profitable life, wonders if there might not be a parallel universe where people like that would "happily live the life they imagined for themselves in their youth."

When the real world turns out to be a lot less friendly than we dreamed it would be, do we give up and settle for what the world is willing to give us without a struggle? Do we rail against God for the unfairness of life? Or do we look deeply into ourselves and only then discover how resilient we are?

As a rabbi, I spent much of my time trying to comfort people for whom life had been harsh, men fired from jobs to which they had faithfully devoted themselves, women whose husbands had left them for no reason other than a flight from middle age, parents of a child killed by a drunk driver. Much of the time, I felt helpless, unable to think of anything to do or say that would heal them. And much of the time, they astonished me with their resilience. It was not that they didn't hurt. It was not that they denied the reality of what had happened to them. They understood that pain and rejection are part of life, and they responded to the shattering of their dreams by saying, I've learned how painful life can be and I want more of it because there is so much in life that is good and I don't want to miss out on it. They came to see the scars on their souls, and sometimes the actual scars on their bodies, not as disfiguring, not as testifying to their being victims, but as battle scars earned in the struggle against the unfairness of life, a struggle in which they were determined to prevail.

It may be that instead of giving us a friendly world that would never challenge us and therefore never make us strong, God gave us a world that would inevitably break our hearts, and compensated for that by planting in our souls the gift of resilience. It was in the harshness of a desert that God, through Moses, forged a band of former slaves into a people on a quest. And it was in a desert that Moses, their leader, found himself challenged daily by the unrelenting complaints of a people who did not always appreciate the destiny to which they had been called.

Robert Frost once wrote,

> *The tree the tempest with a crash of wood*
> *Throws down in front of us is not to bar*
> *Our passage to our journey's end for good*
> *But just to ask us who we think we are.*

The late professor Philip Simmons, a gifted teacher who was debilitated by ALS (sometimes known as Lou Gehrig's disease) at an early age, cites those lines of Frost (from the poem "On a Tree Fallen Across the Road") in his book *Learning to Fall* and goes on to say, "For how many of us has life turned out to be exactly what we had in mind? All of us have at some point faced that tree fallen across the road, all of us have been forced to ask who we think we are." I read recently of a college teacher's homework assignment on the first day of a class for older adults. She asked them to introduce themselves to her by writing two one-page stories about their lives, one of which would begin, "Everything I've ever done has led me to where I find myself today." The second would start, "It is only after many surprises and choices, detours and disappointments, that I have arrived somewhere I could never have anticipated." I doubt that many of us find ourselves, for better or for worse, exactly where we pictured ourselves being ten, twenty, thirty years ago, and I suspect that many of us contemplate where we find ourselves today with a mixture of regret and astonishment.

Professor Simmons recalls vacationing with his family in

New Hampshire one summer and offering to remove some large stones from the dirt road leading to their cabin. His father told him to leave the stones in place. Without them, the dirt road would turn to mud when the rains came. "We need a hard road," his father told him, "not a smooth one."

Joshua Wolf Shenk, in his book *Lincoln's Melancholy*, offers a portrait of Abraham Lincoln as a man weighed down with despair and depression, not only during the years of the Civil War but throughout his life. But the depression did not keep him from living a productive life. On the contrary, it forged a strength of soul that, in the words of the book's subtitle, "fueled his greatness." Shenk writes, "With Lincoln, we have a man whose depression spurred him, painfully, to examine the core of his soul; whose hard work to stay alive helped him develop crucial skills and capacities, even as his depression lingered." His mental condition taught him "to look troubling reality straight in the eye" rather than with unwarranted optimism. Lincoln became a great man and a great president, perhaps the greatest American president ever, because his path to the White House was a hard road, not a smooth one. Like Frost, another man "acquainted with the night," Lincoln used the discouragements of his life not to permanently block his way but to help him discover who he really was. And we, who cannot aspire to be like Lincoln, can be like him in refusing to let the discouragements of our lives permanently deter us from the fulfilling life that may await us.

At the very beginning of the human adventure, Adam and Eve had two children, Cain and Abel. Cain killed Abel and fled, becoming an exile and an outlaw. As far as we know, his parents never saw him again. Despite everything those tragedies taught Adam and Eve about life's ability to break our hearts, they responded to their loss by having a third child, and several sons and daughters after that.

I have known twentieth-century Adams and Eves, men and women who lost their families in the Holocaust, came to America, and had the courage to remarry and begin new families while carrying in their hearts the memories of what had happened to their first families. I have known men and women who were brave enough to risk loving even after having been hurt as a result of making themselves vulnerable to love, who were willing to trust again even after having been betrayed by someone they trusted. Holocaust survivor Elie Wiesel said of Adam and Eve that it is a fine thing to begin, but it is a much greater thing to begin again after what you worked for has been taken from you. At the very beginning of the human adventure, Adam and Eve left this lesson for their descendants who would be emotionally bruised by experience: Life is tough; let's be strong enough not to be broken by it.

How many of us remained for our entire lives in the first job we ever applied for? How many of us went on to marry the first person we ever found attractive and remained married to that person forever? It was only by a process of rejecting and being rejected that we learned who we were and what we were meant to do with our lives.

In 1909, a no-longer-young woman in Manhattan named Henrietta Szold learned that the man she loved and hoped to marry had abruptly gone off and married a woman he had just met. Many a woman in her situation might have withdrawn from the world and immersed herself in self-pity, or perhaps lurched into an inappropriate marriage on the rebound. But instead of wallowing in loneliness, Szold channeled her unrequited love into founding Hadassah, the Women's Zionist

Organization, which over the course of decades inspired millions of Jewish women to do great deeds of love, including saving the lives of children in Nazi-occupied Europe and founding one of the world's leading medical centers in Jerusalem. Unable to find a man to share her love or heal her wounded soul and unwilling to see that love go to waste, she built a worldwide organization to dispense love and healing. When she died, she was buried on the Mount of Olives in Jerusalem, her gravestone reading "Mother of Thousands."

Malcolm Gladwell, writing in *The New Yorker* magazine on the subject of resilience, reports the findings of psychologists who determined that most people are more resilient than we could have expected them to be. The assumption is that people who have been traumatized by sexual abuse, crippling injury, loss of a parent at a young age, or other serious emotional blows will be scarred for life. It turns out that some people are, especially in cases where abuse was repeated or there was reason to feel implicated in causing the traumatic event. But Gladwell cites evidence that most people show an astonishing capacity for emotional healing. They go through a period of anger and/or depression, but most of the time they find their way through it and emerge ready to pick up their lives and go on.

In other words, when life has dealt you a painful blow, let it hurt but trust yourself to get over it. Even as God blessed our physical bodies with recuperative powers, so that, most of the time, most people recover from illness and injury, it would seem that God has blessed our souls with the miracle of resilience, so that most people, most of the time, survive their pain, bear their scars nobly, and manage to go on living, surprising themselves and those around them in the process.

We were all deeply moved by the courage displayed by Christopher Reeve in the nine years following the accident that shattered his near-perfect life and left him paralyzed. We admired his refusal to sink into despair, his unyielding optimism, his commitment to arduous physical therapy. But the most remarkable thing about his story is not that he was able to do it. It is that you don't have to be Superman to do it. Millions of people have been crippled, assaulted, betrayed, or diagnosed with incurable ailments and have responded as courageously as Christopher Reeve did, insisting on going on with their lives and reaching for as much fulfillment and happiness as was available to them. In June 2004, I officiated at the wedding of a woman who spends her waking hours in a wheelchair, having lost the use of her legs to a degenerative disease. It robbed her of mobility, but not of her sense of humor, her courage, or her readiness to enter into married life. Shortly after that, I read the latest book by Stephen Hawking, the British physicist who can barely move or speak but nonetheless continues to revolutionize the world of physics with his insights. I have autographed books for people who attended my lectures but lacked the physical dexterity to shake my hand or the verbal facility to tell me their names or what was wrong with them. But they were able to hold down jobs and form emotional attachments to others. They are not living the life they had looked forward to when they were young, but they are finding happiness and meaning even in the difficult circumstances they find themselves in.

I continue to find proof of the reality of God in the ability of ordinary people to do extraordinary things, and I include not only the afflicted men, women, and children who show such remarkable courage, but the friends, families, doctors, and nurses who respond to them with love and compassion where there might as easily be neglect and resentment. Human beings at their best and bravest continue to amaze me.

How do they do it? Some of them follow Viktor Frankl's dictum that you have more control over what you do about what happens to you than you do about what happens to you. I remember the sixteen-year-old girl who came to see me because she had been diagnosed with juvenile diabetes. It meant a lifetime of medications and injections. It meant cutting back to an extent on the skiing and competitive sports that had been a big part of her life. Most troubling for a teenager, it meant being different from her friends. I said to her that morning, "This is unfair and you don't deserve it. But don't let this one thing define you. Most of you works just fine; there is just one small part of you that's malfunctioning. Try to keep it in perspective." She went on to be an honor student, and thirty-odd years later is a wife, mother, real estate broker, and community leader. That she is also a diabetic is far from the most important thing in her life.

I don't think I could have spoken those words to Christopher Reeve in the days after his accident: "Don't let this one thing define you." What I might have said to him, what he apparently thought of by himself was, Concentrate on what you have left, not just on what you have lost.

In the autumn, when the weather in northern climes turns cooler and the leaves fall from the trees, Jews celebrate Sukkot, the Feast of Tabernacles. Originally a fall harvest festival, the prototype of the American Thanksgiving, Sukkot is observed by building a temporary ramshackle hut and eating our meals in it, as our farmer ancestors in biblical times did at harvesttime. The hut is built to last for the week of the holiday and then be dismantled, but more often than not, the wind and weather save us the trouble of taking it apart by blowing its walls down halfway through the holiday. Jewish law says that even if one or two of the four walls have collapsed, it is still a proper hut in which to observe the festival. I, like many of my colleagues, have preached on that rule: When part of your world has collapsed, make do with what you have left and don't stop celebrating.

Some people, buffeted by misfortune, have found themselves capable of resilience because they did not have to face their problems alone. One of the things that doubles the emotional pain when things go badly is the fear that people will abandon us, either because they see us as deserving punishment at the hands of a righteous God (as one cynical comment puts it, "If you see a blind man, kick him. Why should you be kinder than God?") or because we remind them of their own vulnerability. When the same God who plants the blessing of resilience within us blesses the people around us with the gift of compassion, we are comforted by the knowledge that we have not been abandoned, not by God and not by our friends.

I remember reading many years ago that one of the secrets to living a long and healthy life was to have been seriously ill when you were young. The person who has known sickness early in life will be cured of the illusion of invulnerability, the myth that bad things happen only to other people. (Learning that our son had an incurable illness when he was three years old was that much harder for me to take because I had led a charmed life to that point.) Having known sickness and suffered from it, a person will learn to take care of himself to reduce the chance of it happening again. It may be equally true that the best way to immunize yourself against being crushed by failure and frustration is to experience it at an early age and learn that you can survive it. There is life after failure, and it can be a very satisfying life. Some people who fail early in life will learn to think of themselves as failures. But others will learn that a broken heart is like a broken bone—it hurts terribly but it heals, and, as has been suggested, it often heals stronger at the broken place.

A woman who wanted to tell me how helpful she found one of my books after her husband's death in an automobile accident wrote: "Admitting that I had no choice but to accept what had happened to me was not a statement of defeat. . . . I was giving up the illusion that the circumstances of my life were under my control, a cherished but dangerous notion I had held for a long time and which had at times laden me down with guilt when things didn't go right and I blamed myself." Eulogizing the playwright Arthur Miller, author of *Death of a Salesman* and *The Crucible*, David Mamet wrote in *The New York Times*: "We are freed, at the end of these two dramas, not because the playwright has arrived at a solution, but because he has reconciled us to the notion that there is no solution—that it is the human lot to try and fail. . . . We have . . . laid aside, for two hours, the delusion that we are powerful and wise, and we leave the theater better for [it]." Instead of exhausting ourselves trying to reshape the world to fit our dreams, we are better off using our strength to comfort one another in a world that is almost certain to mock our dreams and break our hearts.

Sometimes the lesson failure brings us is that we need not see failure as a judgment on how competent or deserving we are because no one gets to win all the time and many a loser survives to win another day. Some years ago, I was deeply impressed by an observation in Carol Gilligan's important book

In a Different Voice, to the effect that young boys tend to play games in which you keep score and some win and some lose, while young girls play cooperative games like hopscotch and jumping rope with no winners, no losers, and no bad feelings for having lost. As a result, boys grow up comfortable with competition, with winning and losing, but they are often tone-deaf to another person's feelings about having lost, whereas girls grow up comfortable with sharing and having intimate relationships with others but uncomfortable in settings in which one person has to lose for someone else to win, as if boys were preparing for careers in business and girls for a life of marriage, family, and intimate relationships. (I think that may be less true today than it was when Gilligan wrote it, what with more girls playing soccer and Little League baseball. But I still hear stories about girls not passing the ball to the best player on the team lest she get "too full of herself." And I recall a woman congregant telling me that she had been offered a job selling jewelry from her home and she needed the income but was reluctant to do it because she had a friend who sold jewelry from her home and didn't want to hurt the friend's business. I can't imagine a man being bothered by that.) Gilligan's concern was that the experience of losing was a useful preparation for life, in both personal and business settings, and while the habit of being mutually supportive was wonderful, jump-roping girls might miss out on the experience of losing and surviving the loss. As a result, the first time they lost a competition, whether for a boyfriend, a class election, or a coveted job, they might be devastated.

Kofi Annan, secretary-general of the United Nations, has spoken of how his athletic background taught him to lose without learning to see himself as a loser, a perspective that prepared him for the world of diplomacy. And best-selling author Pat Conroy has written a book about his experience playing on a really bad college basketball team. He called it *My Losing Season*, telling an interviewer: "I've seen winners, guys who have won a national championship, who never got over it, who live continually in the past. A guy on a losing team never does that, because you have to learn to pick yourself up and go forward. It has been great in my writing life. I've seen writers just wilt and suffer under bad reviews. I just think of a bad review as a game I lost." There is always another game tomorrow.

And there is even a sense in which losing can make us stronger. Just as our bodies grow flabby if they are not challenged by hard work and exercise, our souls can grow flabby if they never encounter adversity. The cellist Mstislav Rostropovich is quoted in *The New Yorker* as saying, "Comfort, celebrity are no good for the artist. If Beethoven were alive today, he wouldn't compose a single note, because the people would give him so many sponsorships, corporate gifts, and honorary doctorates. . . . If I had not endured those terrible years [in the Soviet Union], I would have been maybe a good cellist, but not the one I became. Difficult times are necessary for a good performance—the big spill of emotion, from tragedy to enormous joy."

If life did not challenge us, how could we know how strong we are? How would we learn how strong we were capable of becoming? I am not speaking of the sort of disasters that have the power to break us, a terminal illness or a crippling accident, any more than a personal trainer would recommend an exercise so far beyond a client's capacity that it would cause an injury. I have in mind rather the kind of challenge that forces us

65

to choose between giving up in despair or reaching deep inside ourselves for a strength and resiliency we were not sure we had. Psychologist Martin Seligman writes in his book *Authentic Happiness*: "Why were the adults who faced World War II 'the greatest generation'? Not because they were made of different stuff than we are, but because they faced a time of trouble that evoked the ancient strengths within."

Sister Joan Chittister, a talented Roman Catholic nun who yearned to be a novelist, was headed for a graduate program in creative writing at a major university when her order directed her to serve God and the church in a more conventional way. Coming to terms with her disappointment and the loss of her dream, she went on to say in her book *Scarred by Struggle, Transformed by Hope*: "There is no such thing as a life without struggle. . . . There is no one who does not have to choose sometime, some way between giving up and growing stronger. There is no one who has not known what it is to lose in the game of life. . . . The essence of struggle is the decision to become new rather than simply to become older. . . . No one comes out of struggle, out of suffering the same person they were when they went in. Some come out worse, soured on life. Others come out stronger and wiser." As the songwriter Leonard Cohen puts it, "There is a crack in everything; that's how the light gets in."

The first page of the biblical book of Genesis describes God as creating a perfect world, a world where nothing was out of place and everything fit together in complete harmony. "And God saw all that He had made and found it very good" (Genesis 1:31). The last page of the book of Deuteronomy, last of the Five Books of Moses, ends with Moses tantalized by a distant glimpse of the Promised Land and fated to die without ever entering it. Moses, who had served God so faithfully, who had sacrificed so much to lead a stubborn and rebellious people from slavery to freedom, who had brought the word of God down to earth from the mountaintop, will die without achieving either of his greatest desires: he never saw the people become the God-centered community they had been summoned to be, and he would never set foot in the Promised Land he had been looking forward to for forty years, deprived of that privilege for what seems to readers of the Bible to be a trivial misunderstanding. It seems so cruelly unfair. What happened between the first page of the Five Books of Moses with its vision of a perfect world and the last page with its portrait of a faithful Moses denied his life's dreams is that life in all of its messiness, unfairness, and unpredictability intervened, life with its capacity to tantalize us with dreams and then break our hearts.

The most valuable, most enduring lesson we can learn from Moses comes not from his successes but from his failures. It is not about standing up to rulers and demanding justice. It is not about being charitable to the poor or respecting our neighbor's property. It is about facing our past with gratitude and our future with confidence, even as we carry with us the memories of dreams that never came true. There are other, more attainable dreams waiting for us.

4

New Dreams
for Old Ones

We must be willing to get rid of the life we planned
so as to have the life that is waiting for us.

Joseph Campbell

STEVEN Sondheim's 1987 Broadway play *Into the Woods* is a
musical comedy based on familiar fairy tales. The first act
retells the stories of Cinderella, Red Riding Hood, Rapunzel,
and Jack and the Beanstalk pretty much as we heard them when
we were growing up. As the curtain falls to end the act, Cinderella is marrying her prince, Red Riding Hood is safe from
the wolf, and Jack has scampered down the magical beanstalk
after killing the giant and making off with his wealth. Everyone
seems poised to live happily ever after.

But in the second act, we are reminded that most people
don't live happily ever after. Cinderella's Prince Charming turns
out to be a disappointment as a husband ("I was raised to be

charming, not faithful"). The giant's equally giant-sized widow comes looking for revenge. Some characters die, others are left despondent, and no one is particularly happy. The woods of the play's title represent, not only for Red Riding Hood and Hansel and Gretel but for all of us, the dark, uncharted days of our lives where all sorts of dangers lurk.

F. Scott Fitzgerald once wrote that "there are no second acts in American lives." I imagine he meant that once you have messed up your life, you are not given the chance to go back and put things in order. If that is in fact what he had in mind, he was wrong on two counts. First, people who mess up *are* often given a second chance to clean up their mess, a list that would include politicians and athletes who achieve public success after public failure, men and women whose initial business failures are a prelude to business success, and countless husbands and wives who find forgiveness in the wake of wrongdoing and are given the chance to prove that they have learned their lesson. Second, and more to the point of this book, I have known many people whose lives have followed the outlines of Sondheim's play, a glorious and optimistic first act followed by a return to harsh reality in the second.

I think of Moses, basking in the triumphal glow of the Exodus and the parting of the sea, eager to proceed to his people's rendezvous with God, with no way of knowing the frustration, disappointments, and incipient rebellions that await him. I think of all the weddings at which I have officiated, every one of which ended with bride and groom embracing and walking back down the aisle with stars in their eyes and radiant smiles on their faces. Years later, many of them were still comfortably happy with each other and the life they had made, but others had grown to dislike, even hate the people they were married to. Some had separated or divorced; others had settled into patterns of sullen, passionless coexistence. I think of all the young men and women neatly dressed and enthusiastic as they reported for their first day of work, only to find themselves years later demoralized, disillusioned, perhaps even discharged; the anticipated promotions never came, the frustrations multiplied, until they dreaded waking up in the morning and having to go to work. There was a second act and it was an unfortunate sequel to the first.

Some years ago, I read a book by psychologist Daniel Levinson titled *The Seasons of a Man's Life*. It proposed to outline "how every grown man must pass through a series of specific age-based phases which underlie his personal crises, govern his emotional status and attitudes, even shape his behavior." In one arresting phrase, he identified the source of much of the unhappiness in the souls of people halfway through their life's journey. Levinson refers to "the tyranny of the dream." We all start out with dreams of how our lives will turn out—dreams of love, happiness, fame, and fortune. A colleague of mine has written that "a dream is not only our unconscious sorting out the unresolved issues of the day. To dream can imply a sense of a larger vision of life, a sense that things somehow could be better than they are at present." Think of Dr. Martin Luther King Jr. proclaiming "I have a dream" on the steps of the Lincoln Memorial. It is from such dreams that we derive the hope and the energy to commit to a marriage or embark on a career. But when life doesn't match those dreams, what do we do? For Levinson, the only escape from a sense of failure is to free ourselves from the "tyranny of the dream," the conviction that we will have failed at life if our youthful dream hasn't come true.

Maturity, perhaps even survival, requires understanding that "it is no longer essential to succeed, no longer catastrophic to fail."

I had a friend in graduate school who was everyone's choice as "most likely to succeed." Handsome, brilliant, an honors graduate of an Ivy League university, he seemed destined to follow in the footsteps of his very successful and very demanding father. Three failed jobs and two failed marriages later, he tragically took his own life, haunted by the "tyranny of the dream," unable to replace the dream of glorious success with a more realistic, more attainable one.

For the most part, men's dreams center on success in business, women's dreams on fulfilling relationships. Psychological studies have shown that when women are admitted to a hospital for severe depression or a failed suicide attempt, it will almost always be because of a failed or broken relationship— someone important has gone out of a woman's life, through death or rejection. When a man is admitted under the same circumstances, it will almost always be work-related—he was fired, he was passed over for promotion, his company failed, or his stock portfolio evaporated. Teenage girls are driven to thoughts of suicide when boyfriends spurn them or best girlfriends turn on them and they are afraid they will never be loved. Teenage boys contemplate suicide when they feel they have disappointed their fathers, not made the team, not gotten into the right college.

I have never forgotten a conversation I had years ago with a strikingly attractive woman in her early thirties who had just finished interviewing me on the noon news in a medium-sized Southern city and asked if she could talk to me privately after the show. She told me that she had just been offered a job as news anchor in a major metropolitan area, a job she, like most of her colleagues, coveted above all else. The only problem was that she was in a serious relationship with a man in the town in which she lived, and he could not move because he was indispensable to his family's prosperous business in that town. She said to me, "It's the kind of job I dreamed of when I went into this line of work and if I turn it down, in a few years I'll be too old to get another offer like this one. But I really like this guy I'm seeing, more than anyone else I have ever been serious about. My friends who dropped their careers to get married tell me that sometimes they wonder what their lives might have been like had they stuck with their jobs. But my friends who emphasized their careers and still aren't married tell me that they often wake up in the middle of the night panicked at the thought that they might never get married and never have children, and that there will be a terrible void in their lives when they are old and look back at it."

I told her that I had neither the right nor the wisdom to tell her what to do with her life, but the way she put the question reminded me of something a therapist once told me about how to resolve a dilemma. Imagine yourself having grown old and looking back on your life after choosing one path over the other. Then imagine yourself having made the opposite choice. Which scene are you more comfortable with and which one leaves you with more regret? The last thing I heard, she was still at the small-town television station.

I don't know how much of it is in a person's DNA and how much is a social construct, but young women's dreams for the most part center on love, marriage, and motherhood. Most will achieve these goals to a greater or lesser extent, though not always along the lines of their dreams. But the possibility of never marrying or never being a mother can be a source of anguish for many a young woman. It takes a very special strength of spirit to trade in those dreams for dreams more within their reach.

Golda Meir, an American-born woman, was prime minister of Israel in the 1970s. She was a formidable prime minister but a memorably plain-looking woman. (Would anyone ever write a line like that about a male politician?) Meir wrote in her autobiography: "I was never a beauty. There was a time when I was sorry about that, when I was old enough to understand the importance of it. Looking in the mirror, I realized it was something I was never going to have. . . . It was much later that I realized that not being beautiful was a blessing in disguise. It forced me to develop my inner resources. I came to understand that women who cannot lean on their beauty and need to make something on their own have an advantage."

In contrast, I have known good-looking women who used their looks to give them an advantage over others in competing for jobs and husbands, and showed signs of near panic when advancing years threatened to deprive them of that advantage. It was as if they had so completely identified themselves with their attractiveness that, when they began to lose it, they would no longer know who they were.

To the woman who is afraid that she is not attractive enough to win the heart of the man of her dreams, I would suggest that, if the dream she has grown up with is leaving her frustrated and anxious about her future happiness, she might want to trade it in for another dream, one drawn more from reality and less from the pages of romance novels and the plots of Hollywood movies. I would urge her to get over the habit of seeing the dating and mating process as one that equates physical attractiveness with marriage-worthiness. Rather, if you think of yourself as a person capable of loving and deserving love, even if you are not all that attractive by society's standards, shouldn't you be able to see a man who is not all that good-looking as equally capable of loving and equally deserving of being loved, rather than see him (and by implication, yourself) as one of life's losers?

I remember reading about a single woman on a blind date with a young pediatrician. He came across as nerdy and awkward, a shy, stumbling conversationalist who spilled soup on his tie during dinner. The woman was contemplating faking a headache and asking to be taken home early when the doctor's beeper went off. He was called to an emergency and invited her to come along, since it was on the way to her home. Seeing him interact with a sick child, she discovered a tenderness and gentleness in him that surprised her and she began to speculate about what sort of husband and father he might be. If he wasn't the man of her dreams, maybe it was time for her to change those dreams.

It need not be a question of "settling for," of "I don't deserve better." It may be a matter of "there are things I've come to like about myself and even if lots of people can't appreciate them, I only need to meet one person who does."

Some people who yearn for marriage and a family, despite their best efforts, will never marry. It may be a matter of bad timing or too many years of graduate school or job-related travel. It may be bad luck or a matter of simple arithmetic. At a certain age, there are many fewer single men than single women and it is more socially acceptable for the men to seek out younger women. Some people will find themselves drawn to others of the same sex and will encounter legal, religious, or family impediments to turning that attraction into a formal relationship. But that need not condemn a person to what the small-town television personality worried about, the fear of being left with an unbearable void at the center of one's soul. Remember the example in the previous chapter of Henrietta Szold, who never married but found an outlet for her maternal love by founding Hadassah. If few people can be as creative as Henrietta Szold, think of all the aunts (by blood or adoption), teachers, neighbors, and others who are beloved pillars of their communities. If your dream of finding someone who will love you doesn't seem to be coming true, maybe you should dream instead of finding people to love. When you do that, one of two things is likely to happen. Either you will meet the person you will marry once you stop obsessing about it, or else you won't and it won't bother you as much as it once did.

AND THEN there are the people who marry, their hearts and souls filled with dreams of a comfortable home filled with the noise and scattered toys of children, only to have difficulty conceiving and bearing children. For some reason—I have seen it blamed on late marriage, frequent use of contraceptives, polluted air and water—it seems to be more of a problem today than in previous generations (or maybe we are only more aware of it).

In the biblical world, where there was no avenue of fulfillment for a woman other than being a wife and mother, there was perhaps no sadder sentence than "the Lord had closed her womb." It condemned a woman to a life of irrelevance, even divorce and replacement. The book of Genesis speaks of Isaac praying to God on behalf of his wife Rebecca because she was infertile (Genesis 25:21). Rachel, wife of the patriarch Jacob, pleads with him, "Give me children or I shall die" (Genesis 30:1). (Ironically, she is fated to die in childbirth.) The opening chapter of the First Book of Samuel tells of a man who had two wives. One had children whereas the other was childless and was taunted by her rival because of it. Her husband tries to comfort her, telling her that his "love should mean more to her than ten children," but that does not suffice to fill the empty space in her soul, the craving for the ultimate act of creativity, giving birth to a child, which would enable her to say as Eve said, "Like God, I have made a person" (Genesis 4:1). (Interestingly, for the most part, male commentators on the text from First Samuel praise the husband for his tenderness and concern; female commentators criticize him for not hearing his wife's longing for children and for insisting that if she has him, what more does she need?)

This outlook is not confined to ancient Israel. I can recall recent incidents in royal families in the Middle East and Asia where wives were criticized, even replaced, if they could not have children or if they only gave birth to daughters. (Apparently, the educational curriculum for a prince or king does not include high school biology, or they would have learned that 40 percent of fertility problems and 100 percent of gender selection depends on the husband.)

What can we say to all those young husbands and wives yearning for the experience of generating life who encounter only frustration? How do we dry the tears and calm the fears of the woman who fastens on every tentative sign that maybe this month she has succeeded in becoming pregnant, only to be disappointed once again, especially if she is surrounded by friends or by women in the obstetrician's waiting room who are conspicuously pregnant? We can say first that they should be grateful to be living in the twenty-first century rather than a millennium or two ago. There are so many medical miracles today to help infertile couples become parents, from in vitro fertilization to surrogate motherhood. In addition, women today no longer live in a world where being a wife and mother is the only path to fulfillment. In the opening pages of the Bible, there are two accounts of how the first woman was brought to life and named. In Genesis 2:18–23, God fashions a woman to be a companion to the first man because "it is not good for the man to be alone." She is called Wo-man for she was originally the feminine side of the Man. (It is absolutely clear to me that the word *tzela* in Genesis means "side" and not "rib," as I have argued in my book *How Good Do We Have to Be?*.) Then in Genesis 3:20, after the incident in the Garden of Eden, the man names his mate Eve (in Hebrew, *havah*) because she was to be the mother of all human life (in Hebrew, *hai*).

We see then that God's original plan for women was for them to have two dimensions to their identity, two parallel paths to finding fulfillment in their lives, either as individuals seeking and providing companionship or as mothers giving birth to children and taking responsibility for raising them and shaping their souls. If she cannot be Eve, mother of many children, she can be Woman, created to be a friend, a companion, a lover, a person of achievement in her own right.

When the book of Genesis speaks of Abraham and Sarah leaving Haran with their flocks and herds "and the souls they had acquired" (Genesis 12:5), presumably referring to their servants, one commentator takes those words to mean: "Though Abraham and Sarah had been unable to create life to this point, they could create souls by teaching people how to live."

Another states: "When someone teaches a child the purpose of life and shapes his soul, it is as if he or she had given birth to him. Our biological parents give us life in this world; our teachers give us life in time to come."

There is a building in Jerusalem that engages the soul and touches the heart as much as any place on earth. It is called Yad Vashem, the memorial to the victims of the Holocaust. It is an eloquent tribute to the victims of Hitler's brutality, parents and children who were not permitted to live out the full measure of their years. You may have wondered where the name Yad Vashem comes from. In the Bible, God offers these words of comfort to those people who, because they could not have children, fear that their names will perish permanently when they die. God says of them, "I will give them in My house and in My presence a monument and a name [*yad vashem*] better than sons and daughters. I will give them an everlasting name that shall never perish" (Isaiah 56:5). Many people will achieve immortality by having children and grandchildren to bear their name. After our daughter married, I dedicated my next book to her and her husband "who promise me immortality." Others will have an impact beyond their years on earth through the goodness and friendship they shared with those they leave behind. Still others will achieve their immortality, like the victims of the Holocaust, by leaving behind memories of love, courage, and accomplishment in the face of adversity.

THERE is another way in which life at its most unfair breaks the hearts and shatters the dreams of people who yearn for happiness. All too many couples marry and have a child, only to learn at birth or shortly afterward that there is something seriously wrong with their child physically or developmentally. The dreams they nurtured during nine months of anticipation, dreams of seeing him or her grow, dreams of achievement in the classroom or on the athletic field, dreams of seeing their child's first love, departure for college, marriage, and grandchildren are shattered or significantly altered before they could be savored. My wife and I knew that experience when we were told that our three-year-old son had an incurable syndrome that would distort his appearance and severely shorten his life. I know of nothing to match the feeling of helplessness that overcomes a parent at that moment, wishing there were some way you could subtract years from your own life to add to your child's, or that some miraculous medical procedure could transfer some of your own health to him.

There is only one thing a parent can do when that happens: love the child as fully and as desperately as you can. Love the child even if at first it seems he is harder to love than a normal child might be, because he needs that love more than a normal child does. Some years ago, there was a movie titled *Gattaca* starring Ethan Hawke and Uma Thurman. It took place in a futuristic brave new world where science had learned how to create perfect babies in the laboratory, without requiring the sexual coupling of a man and a woman, so that all the uncertainties of gestation could be eliminated, so that all babies would be born strong and bright and healthy and free of birth defects. Then there were people known as "love children" who had been conceived the old-fashioned way and whose genetic perfection could not be guaranteed, so they were treated as second-class citizens. Presumably they were called "love children" because of the manner of their conception, but it occurred to me that they might deserve that label precisely because they ran the risk of being born with serious flaws. A seriously afflicted child has the power to generate a very special kind of love, a love that can redeem his parent from the feelings of resentment and self-pity that such circumstances might otherwise give rise to. The love one feels for a vulnerable child or a retarded or handicapped child is a fiercer, deeper, and more complicated love than the love one feels for a child who earns straight A's and is applying to Harvard. Such a child can pierce the intellectual hard shell that surrounds many a parent's heart and teach that parent to know love and feel pain. I know that because it happened to me.

There is an expression in Judaism, *hesed shel emet,* "authentic kindness." It refers to a good deed done in the knowledge that it will never be reciprocated. Some deeds of kindness can, at least unconsciously, be done with the expectation that the beneficiary will one day do something similar for you. "Authentic kindness" is done without that expectation. The classic example is tending to the needs of the deceased, preparing a body for burial, sitting by its side so that the dead body is never abandoned, accompanying the coffin to the grave. Obviously the deceased will never be able to do the same for you. But loving a seriously incapacitated child, tending to him in his infancy knowing that he may well not be there to tend to you in your old age, would equally deserve to be called "authentic" love.

Then there are the parents whose dreams of seeing their children carry on the family name and standard are cruelly destroyed by a doctor's diagnosis of cancer or a late-night automobile accident. That medical conference, that telephone call from the police, cleaves a family's history into "before" and "after." Like Moses at the foot of Mount Sinai, we are left with the broken pieces of our most cherished dreams lying at our feet. We feel stunned, hurt, angry, and sometimes we feel too shocked, too emotionally paralyzed to feel anything at all. There is so little that well-meaning friends can do at a time like that except to hug the parents and siblings, assure them of our love and support, and then go home and hug our own loved ones more closely because we have been reminded of the fragility of life and of our dreams.

I accepted an invitation to join the national board of MADD, Mothers Against Drunk Driving, to help in their efforts to change the priorities of a society that too often continues to think it is amusing when people drink to excess. A good friend of mine, an emergency room physician, took a year off to work for the Department of Transportation in Washington to help make roads and cars safer and reduce the number of people who will be rushed to emergency rooms. Several members of my congregation, doctors with impressive credentials, have chosen to go into medical research rather than more lucrative private practice in the hope of practicing "wholesale rather than retail medicine," finding cures for the diseases that cut lives short rather than treating sick people one at a time. Life will continue to be painful and unfair, but if by our combined efforts we can spare a hundred families, a thousand families, ten thousand families the pain of having their dreams mocked, it will be holy work.

SOME DREAM of marriage, some dream of children, and life often conspires to thwart their dreams. But I suspect that many of the citizens of the land of broken dreams and disappointment are there because they did get married, they did have children, but they saw the joy and optimism of act I turn into the bitterness and frustration of act 2. What do they then do with that dream? They can cling to it or they can trade it in for a new one.

I am a fan of Anne Tyler's novels about people from the working-class neighborhoods of Baltimore. Tyler has that rare knack of writing about flawed, imperfect people, people with annoying quirks, and making us care about them, even like them. (I remember her account of the family that would not sell their house and move to a nicer one until they had used up all of their return address stickers.) One of her recent novels, *The Amateur Marriage,* tells the story of Michael and Polly Anton, who fall in love in 1942 as Michael is prepared to enlist in the army. They marry a year later, and over the course of decades they grow increasingly dissatisfied with each other, until a small argument tips the scales and they separate and divorce. They are basically good, well-meaning people who married without understanding what marriage was about and, despite trying their best, never quite got the hang of it. They were amateurs. At one point, Anne Tyler imagines Michael thinking to himself: "He believed that all of them, all those young marrieds of the war years, had started out in equal ignorance. He pictured them marching down a city street, as people had on the day he enlisted. Then two by two they fell away, having grown wise and seasoned and comfortable in their roles, until only he and Pauline remained, as inexperienced as ever, the last couple left in the amateurs' parade."

He's wrong, of course. In all likelihood, half or more of the couples who got married when he and Polly did also came to the point of wondering, Who is this person I'm married to and why did I think I would be happy for the rest of my life with this person? Freud once wrote that there are four participants in every marriage: the woman, the man she thinks she is marrying, the man, and the woman he thinks he is marrying. What happens when we realize that the person we are married to is far from perfect and a lot less admirable than we thought? As one man, made wise by bitter experience, wrote, "This realization of the difference between fantasy and reality is the first crisis of a marriage, a crisis every married person faces."

And it's not only about the shortcomings of our mate. It can be about our coming to terms with our own shortcomings as well. A colleague of mine, Rabbi Perry Netter, writing a book about divorce out of the pain of his own failed marriage, suggests that many divorces happen when couples are in their late thirties or early forties, for two reasons. One is that by then the accumulated grievances have reached a critical point, not only in the relationship between husband and wife but in their lives outside of marriage. They may have hit a dead end in their careers. They may be disappointed not only in each other but in their children. Events—an illness, the death of a neighbor— may get them thinking of their own mortality, wondering, Is this all I am ever going to get out of my life? Will I never be happier?

A second factor, the writer suggests, is the extended life span to which people can look forward today. When few people lived much past sixty, a person in his or her forties was likely to think, Why go through all the pain and aggravation of divorce, for myself and the children, in order to end up alone for the last decade of my life? Now that people can realistically expect to live well into their seventies and even eighties, a person can think, I still have almost half of my life ahead of me. Why shouldn't I reach for happiness?

I confess that I have a bias in favor of remaining married to the person you are married to. I believe there were probably good reasons why you married the person you did, and those reasons are still there, buried under the debris of mistakes and hurt feelings. (This does not apply to cases of physical abuse and criminal behavior, which no one should be asked to tolerate.) I believe (and I have seen this happen in so many families) that with a little digging, one can rediscover those feelings. The relationship will probably never be the same. Like Moses, you will go on with your life carrying the broken pieces of the dream you started with. But alongside them, you will also have the intact vision of a new, more realistic, less perfectionist covenant. And I believe that a little humility helps here as well, the ability to see where you may have contributed to the problem and the willingness to tolerate imperfections in your partner as readily as you tolerate them in yourself. One marriage counselor I know would often say to each member of a couple he was advising, "I've heard enough about your complaints about each other. Can you tell me something you've done that has contributed to your unhappiness and something you can do differently to make things better?" For what is love, our love for each other or God's love for us, not to mention Moses' ongoing loyalty to the exasperating people he was called upon to lead, if not the willingness to accept something less than perfection? Psychologist Peter Kramer has written in his book *Should You Leave?*, "There are limits to how different things will be if you exchange this partner for another." If you are mature enough to love someone, you are probably mature enough to love the person you are living with, even if he or she isn't the person you thought you fell in love with and married.

Although I recognize the pain of a disappointing marriage, I also recognize the pain of giving up on a disappointing marriage, the hurt felt by children, the almost unavoidable sense of personal failure, the very real danger of making the same mistake in one's choice of a second partner.

Yet even as I begin with a bias in favor of marriage (spend money on a therapist before you spend it on a lawyer), I recognize, and my religious tradition recognizes, that sometimes relationships die despite one's best efforts, and when they do, there is nothing ennobling about having to live with the decaying remains of a dead relationship. Sometimes a marital choice is a mistake, an unfixable mistake, and when that is the case, maturity means acknowledging the mistake rather than denying it. There will be times when, just as war is never good but is sometimes necessary, marital separation and divorce are sometimes necessary, sometimes the only solution to a failed relationship, even if unavoidably painful. When that happens, the question is not whether to divorce but how.

Rabbi Netter wrote his book in the wake of his own divorce to guide other couples going through the experience. He called it *Divorce Is a Mitzvah*. In Judaism, a mitzvah is a religious obligation, something you do in obedience to God's will as a way of bringing God into your life. By that title, Rabbi Netter was not suggesting that every observant Jew should divorce his or her mate. He was saying that, when divorce does occur, it can be done in a way that will let all parties involved feel that God was present in their parting just as He was at their wedding.

Netter warns that "psychologically, the effects of divorce parallel the trauma of losing a loved one. . . . Deciding to end a marriage is like deciding to amputate a limb. You know there is immense pain in store."

When events cause us pain, there are two things we can do with our pain. We can turn it inward on ourselves and become depressed, or we can turn it outward, convert it into anger, and find someone or something to be angry at (as when we stub our toe in the dark and are angry at the chair for being there rather than at ourselves for walking into it). When the pain is caused by divorce, most people do both. They turn their anger on themselves, condemning themselves as failures for not being able to make their marriage work. Women especially are prone to this, having been conditioned by society to believe that the emotional health of the family is their responsibility. But men are susceptible as well, their sense of competence being tied to succeeding at what they do.

Anne Tyler's Michael Anton laments that he and his wife were amateurs at marriage in the sense that they, like so many of us, committed themselves to it without really knowing what they were getting into. And he is right that he lacked preparation for the role of husband. Just as getting a driver's license doesn't mean that we know how to drive, but that we are ready to gain experience that will help us become good drivers, a marriage license doesn't mean that we are qualified to be a competent wife or husband. It signifies our readiness to learn and, like the student driver, to pray that we don't hurt anyone in the process of learning.

But the word *amateur* has a second level of meaning in addition to suggesting that one is unqualified or inexperienced. *Amateur* comes from the same root as words like *amorous*. It means doing something out of love. The response to the termination of a marriage need not be, I failed because my partner and I were amateurs and didn't know what we were getting into. It can be, I was an amateur at marriage in the sense that I came to it with a heart full of love. The love was real, it was not a mistake, but it turned out that love was not enough to make it work. And at some level, buried under the bitterness and the disappointment, that courage to love is still there if I can only find it. Richard Carlson, author of *Don't Sweat the Small Stuff,* tells of a couple on the verge of separating who are reconciled when the husband is diagnosed with cancer and the wife dedicates herself to caring for him. Carlson asks, Had their love really been lost, or had they merely misplaced it in the stress of daily living?

And alongside the sadness and the sense of failure is the anger. Being angry at our soon-to-be-ex-partner may simply be our way of dealing with the pain we feel. We are angry that life didn't turn out the way we thought it would and we don't know where else to direct our anger except at the person who shared that hope and that disappointment with us. It may be our way of being angry at the outcome of our marriage. It may be a way of shielding ourselves from our share of responsibility for what went wrong. Some of the most disheartening hours I ever spent as a rabbi were times I found myself in the midst of a bitter confrontation between two people who had once loved each other enough to want to share their whole selves with each other: testifying at a court hearing about the religious upbringing of children where a spouse who had converted to Judaism before marriage planned to revert to his or her original religion after the divorce; refereeing an argument between the parents of a thirteen-year-old boy about how his time was to be divided on the afternoon of his bar mitzvah ceremony since the parents would be holding separate parties. Seeing the depth of bitterness and even hatred where there had once been love, I understood why the innermost circle of Hell in Dante's *Inferno* was ice rather than fire.

Rabbi Netter urges us to try not to become defensive in the

face of our partner's anger. If we are the one who made the decision to leave, he would ask us not to respond to the anger with a long list of things our partner did to deserve being left. He would have us realize that the anger "is necessary for your partner's emotional and spiritual healing from the wound caused by being abandoned." It may be unpleasant to be the recipient of anger from someone you once cared deeply about and may still care about. But in almost all cases, anger, pain turned outward, is healthier in the long run than pain turned inward, which leads to depression.

In what sense can one speak of divorce, as Rabbi Netter does, as a *mitzvah,* an opportunity to conjure up the presence of God by our behavior? In a situation that could easily bring out the worst in us, causing us feelings of hatred and dreams of getting even, hurting someone as we have been hurt, God can move us to transcend those feelings that will only embitter our lives. We don't have to turn our pain into anger at another person. We don't have to lessen our pain by hurting someone else (or fantasizing about hurting someone else, which is in some ways worse because then we add helplessness to bitterness). We can turn our pain into sadness that this dream that was once so beautiful and so central to our lives did not come true.

In the most moving and memorable page in his book, Rabbi Netter writes of the day his divorce was finalized. "We stood in the long hallway, and I held Esther as she cried. Ironically, it was while we were separating that we had one of the most powerful moments of intimacy of our entire marriage. Not a word passed between us, but each of us understood the pain in each other's soul. We cried as we hugged each other, and there was holiness in that hug. In spite of the enormous changes I was about to undergo and in spite of the anxiety and fear and enormous pain that those changes were causing, I knew instinctively that I was going to be okay. God was present in that hug, helping us to let go of the anger and disappointment that my life was not going to turn out the way I had planned it."

Perhaps not everyone can bring an unhappy relationship to closure that gently. There will be marriages broken by abuse or betrayal. Yet everyone should try to end a marriage with as little rancor and bitterness as possible, for the sake of everyone involved. Columnist Ellen Goodman puts it this way in her book *Paper Trail:* "The Graceful Exit means leaving what is over without denying its validity or its past importance in our lives. It involves a sense of future, a belief that every exit line is an entry, that we are moving on rather than only moving out." And Sister Joan Chittister writes in *Scarred by Struggle, Transformed by Hope:* "We survive the divorce; will we survive the thought of having been left? We survive the retirement; will we survive the feeling of being useless?"

God blesses some people with happy marriages and healthy children. And God blesses other people with the strength and courage to accept the fact that they will not have happy marriages or healthy children. He helps them to let go of the dream, to free themselves from "the tyranny of the dream," the curse of feeling that life is pointless when dreams don't come true, and to promise them, as He promised Moses on Mount Sinai after the failure of the first set of commandments, that we need not be left with an empty space, a hole in our lives, where the dream once was. There are other dreams to be had.

IF WOMEN (and some men) dream of finding their life's meaning in marriage and parenthood, men (and some women) dream of fame and competitive success. Scientists dream of discoveries that will short-list them for a Nobel Prize, doctors dream of finding cures for diseases, middle managers dream of becoming top executives, athletes dream of starring in the big game, and inventors dream of fashioning a device that will change society for the better. Daniel Levinson writes in *The Seasons of a Man's Life* that a person's dream "is his personal myth, an imaginary drama in which he is the central character, a would-be hero engaged in a noble quest." The reward people envision is not just fame and fortune. It goes deeper than that. The reward that drives their efforts to realize their dream, whether the dream is of business success or exemplary parenting, is the satisfaction of having lived one's life to the fullest and left one's mark on the world. And the corresponding fear is not just disappointment, having to settle for being average and anonymous; it is, in Levinson's words, "a man's worst fear, that he will never realize his potential or—the most terrifying thought of all—that the potential was never really there."

One of the most famous dreams of the last century (in this case, a nighttime dream, though, as we will see, the categories overlap) was the dream psychoanalyst Carl Jung recounts in his autobiography. Jung was one of Freud's most gifted and prominent followers. He became Freud's leading disciple, partly because of his intelligence and intuitive insights into human nature and partly because Freud hoped that Jung's background as the son of a Swiss Lutheran pastor would diminish popular resistance to psychoanalysis as a strictly Jewish enterprise.

Before long, Jung began to have conflicts with Freud. He had his doubts about Freud's emphasis on sexuality as the driving force in human behavior and he resented Freud's inability to accept criticism. It was at this time in his life that Jung had a dream that upset him deeply. He dreamed that he shot and killed Siegfried, the greatest hero of German mythology. Troubled by the dream, Jung called on the principle of dream interpretation that all characters in our dreams are aspects of ourselves. Siegfried, he suggested, represented the ideal of the hero, the wish to do great and glorious things and be cheered by thousands. The message of the dream, Jung concluded, was that he had to slay his soul's craving to be a hero. He had to overcome his desire to become great.

From the first time I read that account, I was suspicious of his interpretation. It seemed just a little self-serving, too innocent an interpretation that shrank from confronting the dream's dark, murderous content. (Full disclosure: I have always been partial to Freud's theories and suspicious of Jung as the Nazi sympathizer who broke the master's heart. That was probably an unfair and ungenerous opinion.) To me, the meaning of the dream was clear. Jung was locked in a struggle with a powerful father figure by the name of Sigmund. He dreamed of killing Siegfried, a thinly disguised variant of Sigmund, as a playing out of the Oedipal conflict, the son/disciple's wish to remove and replace the father.

But some time later, I ran across an obscure fact that led me to believe that Jung may well have been right. I had forgotten something that I suspect Jung knew as well as he knew his parents' first names. In Teutonic mythology, Siegfried is the son of Sigmund, as any fan of Wagner's Ring cycle would know. Dr. David Rosen, in his book *The Tao of Jung,* sees Siegfried as representing Jung's inauthentic self as a loyal follower and surrogate son of Freud. Jung's dream of killing Siegfried represented his way of realizing that his role in life was not to be Sigmund Freud's surrogate son, unquestioningly accepting his teachings, but to painfully declare his independence and find his own way. He had to shed his Freudian identity in order to be true to himself. The dream of a killing, of a sacrifice, was a call to sacrifice his original dream, the dream of being the next Sigmund Freud, and replace it with a more realistic and authentic one. His Siegfried dream moved him to free himself from the harmful influence of his earlier dream, whose message was that he would be a failure if he did not become a world-famous figure.

I have known people who learned that lesson too late, people who were seduced by dreams of fame and influence that led them to pursue an inauthentic goal: excellent lawyers who ventured into politics, losing their earlier careers without gaining a new one, or worse, compromising their souls in the process; competent salesmen who went into business for themselves and found they were beyond their depth; rabbis and ministers who left congregations where they were beloved to accept the call to a more prestigious, and more fractious, church or synagogue. Sometimes it worked out well and people found the fulfillment their souls craved, the success they dreamed of. But at least as often, their dream led them astray. For every one who dared and succeeded gloriously, there were more who dared equally boldly and failed.

It is a hard thing to predict in advance. I have known too many people who followed their ambition off a cliff and had to live with the wreckage of their dream and a diminished sense of their own abilities. I have known others who, to an outside observer, seemed to have succeeded, but at the cost of their authenticity. They succeeded by becoming someone other than who they knew deep down they really were. I have known women who translated impressive talent and hard work into a position of major responsibility at their company, only to learn that, in order to succeed at their new job, they would have to become just as ruthless, just as neglectful of their families as their male colleagues were. Regardless of how things turned out, they felt they were being forced to turn into someone other than who they really were. Those clergymen and -women who moved to a larger, more prominent church or synagogue, the fulfillment of their professional dream, too often found out that their new position demanded they be less of a pastor and more of an administrator/politician/ fund-raiser. Business executives would tearfully tell me how much they hated their jobs but were trapped by the prospect of losing pensions, lowering their family's standard of living, and facing the question, Where do I go if I walk away from a job like this?

And then there were people who, for one reason or another, resisted the seductive call of the inauthentic self. Some were reluctant to give up a situation in which they were reasonably happy in exchange for the possibility of glorious success or spectacular failure. (Economists have learned that the average person's economic decisions are more strongly influenced by the fear of losing what one already has than by the hope of gaining something he or she lacks.) Others intuitively understood that the position dangled before them was a very attractive one but was not for them. They would have had to become someone else for that suit to fit.

At the beginning of the service on Yom Kippur, the Day of Atonement, the congregation prays for forgiveness "for all of us and for the stranger, the alien in our midst" (Leviticus 16:29–30). The reference was originally to any visitor who might have attached himself to the congregation for this service. But one commentator offers a deeper understanding of the phrase. He suggests that every one of us has a stranger, an alien identity, in our midst, an inauthentic self that keeps trying to persuade us to do things that are not truly us. On the Day of At-One-Ment, we need to be cleansed of that alien, inauthentic soul.

Jung's life-altering experience can teach us that sometimes the most useful dream is the one that calls on us to give up the dream we have been chasing, the dream our parents had for us and consciously or unconsciously bequeathed to us, the expectation society imposed on us. Mariana Caplan writes in her book *The Way of Failure,* "Have we failed in our pursuit of happiness, or have we been chasing an incorrect notion of happiness, one that was doomed to fail?"

DR. ROSEN uses the word *sacrifice* in reference to Jung's giving up his seductive but ultimately inauthentic identity as Freud's disciple. In baseball, a sacrifice refers to a batter giving himself up to help the team. It is an admirable act but not a particularly painful one; it doesn't even count against the player's batting average. But in the Bible, and in real life away from the baseball diamond, *sacrifice* means a lot more than giving something up. *Sacrifice* (from the Latin, meaning "to make holy") means fashioning a moment of holiness by giving something away. It means giving up something important to you in an effort to draw closer to God. The biblical term for sacrifice comes from a root meaning "to draw near by bringing (the offering) close." Thus the Bible forbids bringing lame animals, animals captured in the wild, and unripe, inedible fruit as an offering; they do not represent a giving up of anything meaningful. A sacrifice is not a bribe to God to ingratiate yourself with Him. The Bible tells us repeatedly that God does not need animal offerings for His nourishment nor is He impressed by the flattery that accompanies them. The purpose of the sacrifice is *for us to divest ourselves of things that we think we need in an effort to let our true selves emerge.* The person who gives generously to charity discovers that he or she does not really need the money given away as much as he or she needs the sense of having made the world a more compassionate place. People who devote time to a worthy cause find themselves no less capable of getting necessary work done. If anything, they feel enriched by the discovery of how much they can do without.

There comes a point in a person's life, Daniel Levinson writes in *The Seasons of a Man's Life,* when his or her "basic orientation toward success and failure normally begins to change. It is no longer crucial to climb another rung on the ladder, to write another book, get another promotion, earn more of the rewards that meant so much in the past. . . . He sees that the hero is a youth who must die or be transformed as early adulthood comes to an end. A man must begin to grieve and accept the symbolic death of the youthful hero within himself [and learn to] be a hero of a different kind." Where we once thought that happiness meant realizing our dream, we come to understand that happiness may mean giving up the dream and exchanging it for one that fits us better.

The biblical book of Leviticus describes Moses instructing the Israelites about the varieties of sacrifice that were available to them in various circumstances. Scholars believe that Leviticus was originally a technical manual for priests, telling them when, how, and where to perform the sacrificial rituals, which is why it is so filled with obscure technical language. The first chapter of Leviticus tells us "when a person brings a bull as an offering . . . When a person brings a sheep . . . When a person brings a pigeon . . ." Then, at the beginning of the second chapter, there is a slight but significant change in vocabulary. Speaking of the offering of flour and oil, the poor person's offering, instead of using the word *adam,* "a person," the verse reads *nefesh,* "when *a soul* brings an offering." What kind of sacrifice does a soul make? When a person gives up an unworthy or unrealistic dream that has motivated him or her for years, when we finally free ourselves from the tyranny of the dream, that is the sacrifice our soul brings to God's altar. When a man or woman comes to realize that he or she can achieve the dream of fame and wealth only by neglecting one's family and compromising one's integrity and reluctantly decides that it is not worth it, that is the sacrifice our soul makes. When a young man realizes that the goal he has spent years pursuing, be it medical school or a career as a professional athlete, is really his father's dream and not his (did Cain become a tiller of the soil to fulfill his father Adam's dream of reclaiming the Garden of Eden?), and chooses to disappoint his father rather than compromise his own integrity, that is the sacrifice a soul makes. When a woman comes to terms with the sad truth that she is likely never to be a mother and channels her love into teaching, social work, or some form of community service, that is the sacrifice offered by her soul. There will be reluctance, there will be sadness and pain, the pain of giving up something that was an important part of her for so long. But, done right, there is holiness in that gesture too. Thomas Moore, author of the best seller *Care of the Soul,* writes in his book *The Soul's Religion:* "Life gives us plenty of opportunities to make sacrifices. Getting a divorce or changing jobs may entail the kind of sacrifice that increases the holiness of one's life, depending on how we handle it. . . . Secularism is life without sacrifice."

What do we do with the dreams we have learned we must shed? Can we simply discard them as the embarrassing fantasies of immature youth? I don't see how we can or why we should. They were too much a part of us for too many years for us to pretend we never dreamed those dreams. When life gives us the inevitable message that our marriage will not be the "happily ever after" we hoped it would, that our children will be other than who we dreamed they would be, that our careers will grind to a halt somewhere short of our imagined goal, and that the only road to sanity and happiness involves freeing ourselves from the tyranny of those dreams and the feelings of failure that accompany their nonfulfillment, what do we do then?

We do what Moses did when he realized that his dream of teaching people to walk in God's ways would not be realized as easily as he had hoped, when the shattered fragments of the commandments written by the hand of God lay in pieces at his feet. He lovingly gathered up the pieces of his broken dream and for the rest of his life carried them with him in the same Ark in which the whole stones of the replacement tablets rested. I can imagine Moses saying to himself as he contemplated those fragments touched by the hand of God, Those broken pieces of stone remind me that I had a dream once, a dream of how I would reshape the world, a dream of how God, working through me, would make everything perfect. It didn't turn out that way. But those stones speak to me not of failure and frustration but of reality, of the limits of what is possible when you are working with human beings. I ended up using them as stepping-stones, building blocks that helped me learn about human nature, about myself and other people, about realistic and unrealistic hopes. Rather than giving up on life, rather than giving up on people because of my disappointment, I built on the experience of my disappointment. The broken tablets pointed me toward wholeness, and the dream that didn't come true helped me discover where truth lies.

Broken dreams, broken hearts, hopes unrealized should not be seen as emblems of shame, badges of failure. If anything, they are tokens of courage. We were brave enough to dream, brave enough to long for so much, and when we did not get it, we were brave enough to carry the fragments of those dashed hopes with us into the future, telling us who we used to be as a prelude to our discovering who we might become.

5

Keeping Promises

THERE is a moment in the biblical account of the Exodus that never fails to move me. The last and most devastating of the Ten Plagues, the striking down of the firstborn son in every Egyptian family, has finally broken Pharaoh's resistance and, in the middle of the night, he agrees to let the Hebrews go free. They rush to prepare to leave, not even taking time to bake bread for the journey, which is why to this day Jews commemorate the Exodus by eating matzo, flat unleavened bread, during the week of Passover. The Egyptians give them presents of gold, silver, and fabrics, either out of eagerness to see them gone or out of guilt for how they had treated them, gifts that would be used to fashion the Ark and the Tabernacle in the wilderness. And then we read, "Moses took with him the bones of Joseph, who had exacted a promise from the Israelites on his deathbed, saying 'When God takes note of you, you shall carry my remains from here with you' "(Exodus 13:19).

I love that scene. All around him, people are trying to stuff as much into their luggage as they can, and Moses is busy keeping a promise. Moses shows his greatness in that moment by choosing to keep a promise rather than to enrich himself.

We need to understand the specialness of Moses at that moment because one day you will stand at a crossroads in your life when you will have to choose between personal gain and keeping a promise. There may well be moments when the only way to achieve your heart's desire and make your dreams come true will require your breaking a promise you had made to someone, possibly even a promise to yourself. What will you do at a time like that? Will you keep the promise or break it in the quest for personal advancement? Keeping the promise will be a sign of your inner strength and mature humanity.

The Dybbuk, a classic play of the early-twentieth-century Yiddish theater, tells the story of two young men who are best friends. They both marry and the two wives become pregnant shortly afterward. The two friends swear an oath to each other that if one has a son and the other a daughter, their children will marry so that their friendship will be cemented for eternity. One does have a son, the other a daughter, and they promise each other that when the children come of age, they will be betrothed to each other.

Life takes the two friends in different directions. The one with a son becomes a scholar, as does his son after him. The other becomes a wealthy merchant and soon forgets about his oath to his friend. As you might expect in a play, the two young people meet and fall in love. The wealthy father forbids their marrying, having a more prestigious groom in mind for his daughter. The scholar's son dies of a broken heart, and his ghost enters the body of his beloved, taking it over. This is the dybbuk, the alien spirit of the play's title.

While the merchant-father is waiting for the rabbis to arrive to exorcise the alien spirit, a mysterious stranger approaches him and says, "May I ask you a question? Look out the window and tell me what you see." The merchant says, "I see people." "Now look in the mirror and tell me what you see." "I see myself." "Isn't that interesting," the stranger says. "The window is glass and the mirror is glass. But the glass in the mirror is covered by a thin coat of silver. And as soon as the silver enters the picture, people stop seeing each other and can only see themselves." The merchant realizes that this calamity has befallen his family because greed led him to break a promise to a friend.

To my mind, it says something very troubling about our society that we all too often assume that a political candidate who makes lavish promises while campaigning for office will forget them or give them a low priority once elected. It is as if we and the candidate have agreed to participate in an electoral charade in which candidates cannot be held responsible for what they say on the campaign trail any more than movie actors can be held personally responsible for what they say or do on the screen. Yet what happens to a society when we have virtually given up expecting men and women in high office to take their promises seriously? What happens to the level of mutual trust throughout society when a giant corporation declares that profits have fallen and as a result they will no longer honor their promises of job security, health insurance, or pension benefits?

Is that piece of green paper we call a five-dollar bill really worth five dollars? The only thing that makes it more valuable than a bit of Monopoly money is a promise by the government that it is in fact worth five dollars, no more and no less. Terrible chaos would ensue if we stopped believing in the government's will and ability to keep that promise. That is what happened in Germany in the 1930s, when people's faith in the government was so weak that they felt they had to rush to the market with a wheelbarrow full of rapidly depreciating currency, to buy anything they could before the value of their paper money dropped further. But as our cynicism about politicians keeping their word increases, the very basis of our social life becomes that much more fragile.

We are as vulnerable to being hurt by private breaches of faith as we are by public ones. I once read a letter to the advice columnist in the newspaper in which a woman described how, after twenty years of a stable and gratifying marriage, her husband received a phone call from an "old flame." He had been deeply in love with this woman in college, but she broke his heart by marrying someone else. Now she showed up, newly divorced, and was "just wondering how he was getting along." Since the phone call, the husband has had several long phone conversations with this woman and met her once for lunch, "just to listen to her problems as anyone would do for an old friend." The wife is concerned that her husband has never entirely gotten over the dream of this woman loving him and he may be tempted to break his marriage vow to "forsake all others," to pursue this old flame and revive a half-forgotten dream.

I remember reading the story of a compulsive gambler who swore to his wife and teenage daughter that he was finished making their lives miserable by gambling away their household money, but he could not resist the temptation of a "big score" that would more than make up for all the money he had lost over the years. So he broke his promise, took money out of his daughter's college savings account, and of course lost it all.

In all too many cases, a person who is not strong enough to give up the dream that he once believed would make him happy, even if it means breaking a promise he made to people he cares deeply about, will end up hurting people he loves.

Keeping a promise is more than just maintaining your own integrity. It is more than doing what you said you would do. It is a sign that you recognize the image of God in another person by taking your obligation to that person as seriously as you take your own well-being. When the psalmist tries to define the good person, the person of integrity, by asking the rhetorical question "Lord, who may live in Your presence? Who may dwell on Your holy mountain?" one of the characteristics of the good person is "he takes an oath to his own harm and does not change it" (Psalms 15:1, 4).

I have a friend, a successful attorney, who is a classic-movie fan. When I first met her, she asked me, as I gather she asks all new acquaintances, what my favorite films were. I named two of the usual suspects for someone of my generation: *Casablanca* and *Shane*. She shook her head in dismay. "What is it with you men? You always go for the movie where the hero walks away from the woman who loves him. Women love movies where the guy and the girl come together at the end. Men prefer movies where the hero chooses his freedom over life with a wonderful woman who is smitten with him— Humphrey Bogart sending Ingrid Bergman off to Lisbon because he would rather remain in Nazi-occupied Morocco than leave with her. I mean, really! Fighting Nazis rather than living with a young Ingrid Bergman. Alan Ladd riding off alone while young Brandon de Wilde cries after him, 'Come back, Shane. We love you. Momma loves you.' Do you men really prefer not being tied down to someone rather than having a genuine, permanent relationship?"

I told her: "I think you're missing something. Yes, they turn their backs on women, beautiful women who love them and want to be with them. *But those women are married to someone else.* In fact, in both of those films, they are married to men whom the hero admires. Bogart doesn't exactly reject Bergman at the end of *Casablanca.* He sends her off to join her husband who is a hero of the anti-Nazi resistance. He makes it clear that he loves her but recognizes that she belongs to someone else. Alan Ladd in *Shane* recognizes that Jean Arthur is taken with him, but he has come to admire the quiet, stubborn courage of her husband, played by Van Heflin, too much to break up their family. Those men are not fleeing commitment. On the contrary, they are honoring commitment, someone else's commitment. In fact, if you want to speculate further, both husbands are older men who function in a way as father figures to Bogart and Ladd. There is almost a whiff of an Oedipal situation there: the young man loves a woman who loves him in return but he recognizes that a powerful older man has a prior claim to her and he agrees to give her up. It's not all that different from what Meryl Streep does at the end of *The Bridges of Madison County,* when she spurns the offer of an exciting, passion-filled life with Clint Eastwood because she feels it would be wrong for her to leave her husband." Like Moses at Joseph's burial place, Streep's character chooses to keep a promise rather than break it to reach for personal gain. Like the person of integrity pictured in the Fifteenth Psalm, she has taken an oath and will keep it, whatever the personal cost.

"Get it in writing" is the advice of the experienced to the innocent, the implication being that people are out to cheat you and you have to watch out for yourself. You can't count on people to keep their promises. (Or as the legendary movie producer Sam Goldwyn is supposed to have said, "Oral commitments aren't worth the paper they're written on.") During our daughter's senior year in high school, we bought her a used car, more to liberate ourselves from carpooling than to make her life easier. Because the people selling it insisted that we sign an agreement stating we were buying it "as is," we had it checked out by a mechanic friend who test-drove it and pronounced it safe and serviceable. After our daughter had driven it for a week, it developed problems. It turned out that the sellers had disconnected the wire leading to one of the "trouble" lights that would have indicated problems with the alternator. It would have cost as much to fix it as we had spent on the car. We sold it at a loss and considered it part of our daughter's education: not everyone keeps his or her word. Increasingly, our working and shopping encounters with strangers, people we have never seen before and may never see again, are rooted in suspicion rather than trust. Why should strangers keep their word when they can increase their profit by breaking it?

By contrast, the diamond industry is run almost entirely by Orthodox Hasidic Jews and transactions are sealed by a handshake and a Hebrew blessing. The diamond merchants believe that God takes note of their business practices. They also understand that even a rumor of dishonesty would put them out of business. They have a practical as well as moral reason to keep their promises.

Father Joseph Greer spent many years as a Catholic priest in the Boston suburb where I live. He died all too young, and the

story of his battle against terminal illness has been told beautifully by Paul Wilkes in the book *In Mysterious Ways*. Father
Greer once told me that when he interviewed a couple at
whose wedding he would be officiating, he would say to them,
"Is there anything you're going to be doing after you get married that maybe you ought to start practicing now so that you'll
be good at it?" The couple would usually blush and the
prospective groom would typically say, "I don't know what
you're thinking of, Father, but if it's what I'm thinking of, we're
pretty good at it already." Father Greer would reply, "I don't
know what you're thinking of. I was talking about keeping
promises." The foundation of a solid marriage is the trust that
two people have in each other to live up to the promises they
made to each other at their wedding.

When a husband or wife betrays those promises, the biblical
term for that is *adultery*. In today's parlance, we tend to trivial-
ize the seriousness of it by referring to it as "an affair" or "fool-
ing around," as if it were no more than the discreet pursuit of
fun. Fan magazines carry accounts of the couplings and uncou-
plings of celebrities. Businessmen seem offended that anyone
should object to what they do in their private lives. But a more
serious equivalent of the biblical term *adultery* is *infidelity*, not
being faithful, not being a person who can be counted on to
keep one's word, a person in whom one can have faith. It's not
the sex that is the sin in an act of adultery, it is the failure to take
one's promises seriously.

After the Covenant at Sinai had been sealed, God summoned Moses to spend forty days with Him atop the mountain
to receive the hundreds of rules of behavior that go beyond
the Ten Commandments. (As one scholar puts it, "The Ten
Commandments—don't murder, don't steal—are a prescrip-

tion for staying out of jail. But for a life of holiness, there is a lot more you have to do or not do.") It was toward the end of those forty days, as we remember, that the Israelites built a Golden Calf and celebrated it as "the God who brought us out of Egypt." When Moses saw this, he broke the tablets he had been carrying down the mountain, scolded the Israelites harshly, and then administered a strange punishment. He had the calf ground into powder, mixed the powder with water, and made the people drink it (Exodus 32:20). Why this bizarre punishment? Later in the Torah, we encounter this ritual again. In chapter 5 of the book of Numbers, we read of the ordeal of the wife suspected of being unfaithful. If a husband has suspicions about his wife's fidelity but has no proof, he brings her before the priest who mixes earth from the floor of the sanctuary with water, writes a curse on a piece of paper, dissolves the paper in the water, and makes the woman drink it, telling her that if she is innocent, nothing will happen, but if she is in fact guilty of what the husband suspects, the potion will make her ill. Most scholars see this as a case of psychosomatic reaction; a woman with a guilty conscience will believe the priest and make herself sick. I have always suspected that the ritual was in fact a charade to convince the husband to set aside his suspicions and take his wife back. Whereas a verdict of "not guilty in the absence of proof" might not have convinced him, a sign from heaven declaring his wife innocent should be persuasive.

But for purposes of our discussion, the similarity between the ordeal in Numbers 5 and the punishment inflicted on those who worshipped the Golden Calf suggests that Moses was enraged by what the Israelites did, not because they were worshipping an idol but because they had broken a promise. In the Bible, the punishment for idolatry is death, and Moses does call for the execution of several thousand ringleaders (Exodus 32:28). Drinking the foul water is the punishment not for idol worship but for unfaithfulness, and for Moses, that was the sin of the people who gave themselves over to idol worship. It is as if he were saying to them, I don't expect you to be perfect. I don't expect you to be free from transgression at all times. But is it too much to expect you to live up to what you have promised?

Keeping one's promise is the cornerstone of a sense of responsibility, and I have long considered responsibility for one's behavior to be the defining characteristic of a mature human being. That is why we don't hold pets or little children accountable for losing things or breaking things. They have not attained a level of responsibility.

Randy Cohen writes a weekly column called "The Ethicist" in *The New York Times Magazine.* People write to him with ethical dilemmas, and he gives them advice. I usually find myself agreeing with him, often impressed by his reasoning. But every now and then, I put down my Sunday paper feeling that Cohen has gotten it wrong. One Sunday, he printed a letter from a reader in California with the following problem: "My ten-year-old son and I submitted a form to our synagogue reserving a date for his bar mitzvah ceremony. It included our commitment for him to continue his religious education through tenth grade. He is willing to do so but cannot truly commit to behavior five years from now, and I won't force him to. Was it ethical for us to sign this commitment?"

Cohen answers in part: "Having made a sincere declaration of your intention to continue, you behaved honorably. If in the future you or your son amend your ideas about his Jewish studies, that is understandable and reasonable." My feeling that

Cohen dropped the ball on this one is not just a matter of wanting youngsters to continue learning about their religion. Neither of the synagogues I have served ever demanded such a pledge. My disappointment goes deeper than that. I would have urged the father to take advantage of the pledge issue as a "teachable moment," an opportunity to teach a youngster on the cusp of adolescence and about to enter the world of adult responsibility (that's what becoming a bar mitzvah is all about) that the foundation stone of being a responsible person is one's readiness to keep a promise. That is the difference between the person who has grown up and matured and the person who has only grown older. I can't think of anything more destructive to the soul of a young adolescent than to have his father tell him, If you promise someone something and then change your mind, that's all right—you don't have to keep your word. People take out bank loans, craftsmen accept deposits to do work, and most significantly people get married on the expectation that both parties will live up to what they promised. In the same way that no one is allowed to drive a car without demonstrating the ability to negotiate traffic and parallel park, no one should be permitted to marry or start a business without having demonstrated the readiness to keep his or her word.

Real men keep promises. Strong women keep promises. Public officials deserving of our vote keep promises. People who want others to take them seriously keep promises. Several years ago, there was an awkward incident in which a Chicago-area synagogue threatened to take one of its members to court to compel him to pay a pledge he had made to the temple's building fund. The man had promised a large sum of money and had been publicly honored for it, but he never paid the pledge. He claimed business reverses; the synagogue accused

him of living lavishly. (The executive director of a large synagogue once told me of saying to a temple member, "You've got
two new cars and a boat in your driveway, a live-in maid, and
you've just returned from a vacation in the Caribbean. How
can you tell us that you can't afford to pay your children's religious school tuition?" The man answered, "If you had just
bought two cars and a boat and taken a vacation in the
Caribbean, you wouldn't be able to pay your bills either.") The
synagogue's action may have been unwise and the resulting
publicity probably didn't do their membership campaign much
good, but I could see their point. It wasn't only that they were
counting on the money. Churches and synagogues are in the
business of teaching people to keep their promises—their
marriage vows, their business commitments, their promises to
themselves and to God about changing aspects of their behavior. The most solemn moments in the entire Jewish liturgical
year come on the eve of Yom Kippur, the Day of Atonement.
We begin the twenty-four-hour period of prayer and fasting by
asking God to forgive us for all the promises we made in good
faith during the past year that, despite our best efforts, we were
unable to keep. We don't want to come before God on that day
of judgment as people who don't care about keeping promises.
We don't want to enter the new year thinking of ourselves as
people who don't keep promises. We understand that every
time we break a promise, every time we tell a lie or revert to
a bad habit we vowed to break, something inside us, our integrity, breaks as well. On Yom Kippur, the Day of Atonement,
the day of becoming one, becoming whole instead of being
broken, we pray for the ability to knit our broken souls together so that we will be able to do what we said we would do
and become the people we swore we would be.

Many years ago, I met with a young couple who would be getting married in my synagogue. I wanted to get to know them better and tell them some things about the Jewish wedding ceremony (like the fact that, in Judaism, the bride doesn't have to be "given away" by her father or some other male authority figure). Everything was going well until the prospective bridegroom asked me: "Rabbi Kushner, would you be willing to make one small change in the ceremony? Instead of pronouncing us husband and wife till death do us part, could you pronounce us husband and wife for as long as our love lasts? We've talked about this, and we both feel that if we ever get to the point where we no longer love each other, it's not morally right for us to be stuck with each other and be deprived of any chance for happiness."

I told the couple, No, I wouldn't agree to that change. I told them that I respected their distaste for hypocrisy, for not wanting to live in a loveless marriage. I told them that I could understand their fear of making a total commitment to this marriage because it might hurt too much if it didn't work out. But I warned them that if they didn't enter this marriage on the assumption that it was for keeps, if they moved in together but didn't totally unpack, ready to move out when things got tough, there was no chance that they would be happy together. They would not be committed enough to stay together during the inevitable rough times.

Judith Viorst, in her book *Grown-up Marriage,* has written: "In a grown-up marriage, we recognize that we don't always have to be in love with one another. . . . But a grown-up marriage enables us when we fall out of love with each other to stick around until we fall back in." That is, one of the promises a husband and wife make to each other is the commitment to stick together through the hard times in the faith that the hard times will one day end and the affection they once felt for each other will reemerge.

A 2005 newspaper article described how several European countries are experimenting with legally recognized relationships, sometimes called registered partnerships or civil solidarity pacts, that would offer most of the benefits of marriage without the sense of permanency, or at least the difficulty involved in leaving, that marriage implies. These have nothing to do with the civil unions offered to gay couples in some jurisdictions. They are for heterosexual couples who want to be formally connected to each other by something less permanent, less binding than marriage. That bothers me. I respect the fact that many couples would opt for a registered partnership as a way of saying that there was more to their relationship than just reciprocal sexual availability. But my concern is that a relationship that is relatively easy and painless to get out of leaves each party constantly asking, Are my needs being met or would I be happier elsewhere? rather than asking, Am I doing enough to meet my partner's needs? Judith Viorst writes, "I hear from marital therapists and divorce attorneys that many spouses who choose to end their marriages could, with more effort and sacrifice, maybe a great deal of effort and sacrifice, preserve them." In *Childhood and Society*, Erik Erikson defines intimacy as "the capacity to commit oneself to a relationship and the ethical strength to abide by that commitment despite significant sacrifice and compromise." My own bias, as I said earlier, has always been to counsel couples to give their current marriage every chance to be rehabilitated. We can't always run away from ourselves; much of the time, we find our selves following us.

Some years ago, a best-selling book on relationships urged its readers to look out for themselves first and seek their own self-fulfillment, and if that meant hurting other people in the process, well, let it be a growing experience for them, a lesson in how life works. I thought that was a very wrong message to send people. I will readily acknowledge that it is often hard, sometimes virtually impossible, to tell the difference between healthy self-fulfillment and narcissistic selfishness, between "I am suffocating and being exploited in this relationship" and "I wonder if I could be happier with someone else." But my personal and pastoral experience has taught me that one of the key components of self-fulfillment is letting other people into your life, learning to see their needs and their feelings as being as legitimate as your own. You are not really a mature adult until you learn that.

David Brooks wrote a *New York Times* column on the subject of husbands and wives maintaining separate checking accounts, in the course of which he recalled a Tolstoy novella titled *Family Happiness.* In it, a wife, after several years of marriage, realizes the change that has taken place in her relationship to her husband. "That day ended the romance of our marriage . . . but a new feeling of love for my children and the father of my children laid the foundation for a new life and a quite different happiness, and that life and happiness have lasted to the present day." Brooks went on to write: "Tolstoy's story captures the difference between romantic happiness, which is filled with exhilaration and self-fulfillment, and family happiness, built on self-abnegation and sacrifice. . . . Public life is individualistic. It is oriented around goals like *self*-development, *self*-advancement and *personal* happiness. . . . The goal of family life, on the other hand, does not revolve around individual choices but around the unconditional union of souls. When we get married, and then when we have kids, we learn, sometimes traumatically, to say farewell to the world of me, me, me."

I am well aware of the fact that many marriages don't work out. Some were mistakes from the start, prompted by unplanned pregnancy or young people desperate to leave home. In other cases, people who might have been well matched at the outset grow in different directions (as a chess grand master said of his ex-wife, "We had become bishops of different colors") or are victimized by a tragedy that finds the hidden fault line in a relationship. And I have seen many second marriages work out beautifully. People are more mature, more realistic. But while it is realistic to know as you get married that there is such a thing as divorce and that it is no longer stigmatized as it once was, and that no one should be compelled to live with the corpse of a dead relationship, it is *always* a mistake to enter marriage with an attitude of, Let's try it; if it doesn't work out, we'll just go our separate ways, with no hard feelings. Because the promises we make at our weddings have a more serious impact on the lives of other people than any other commitments we make, because marriage is more like a covenant and less like an economic or sexual agreement, we owe it to ourselves, to our sense of our own integrity, and to those other people to take those promises seriously. That, I suspect, is why so many people who may not otherwise think of themselves as religious feel the need to have a church or synagogue wedding rather than a perfunctory civil ceremony. They understand the awesome solemnity of what they are doing. Author Thomas Moore has written in *The Soul's Religion* that many marriages are failing today "because we treat them as sociological constructions or psychological arrangements rather than as holy mysteries."

Diane Rehm is the host of a popular radio talk show heard in many cities on National Public Radio. I have appeared on her program to discuss several of my books and have always found her a most thoughtful interviewer. Several years ago, she and her husband, John, wrote a revealing, movingly honest book about their marriage titled *Toward Commitment*. At one point, John pays tribute to Diane, writing, "Your almost irrational commitment to the relationship is what sustained our relationship at its darkest moments . . . [otherwise] there is a good chance I would have walked away." He goes on to say, "I thought one got married, had children and the new co-existence automatically created a family. . . . Diane taught me that if a genuine family is to be created, it takes work, it takes thought, it takes a constant determination to keep this often fragile entity called a family together." Asked what kept them together, he answers, "If it was love, it was love of a very unromantic kind. *It was a love composed of loyalty and stubbornness*" (my italics). Diane adds: "Any relationship at times involves just sticking it out, no matter how difficult those times are. It was at a time in this country when divorce was occurring frequently and people accepted the idea that if your marriage doesn't work, you move on to someone else. But I wasn't about to be a serial marrier."

Their exchange reminds me of that scene in *Fiddler on the Roof* where Tevye asks his wife of twenty-five years, "Do you love me?" She answers that for her, love is not a matter of starry-eyed, romantic ecstasy. Love means putting up with her often exasperating husband because that is a commitment she made long ago and because the things they have shared together are too much a part of her identity to be painlessly amputated. A congregant once told me that she probably had sufficient justification to leave her husband but "I couldn't handle the thought of someone walking around out there unconnected to me but carrying half of some of the most intimate memories I possess."

When some unsavory details about President Clinton's personal behavior came to light, many people wondered why his wife, Hillary Rodham Clinton, didn't leave him. All sorts of cynical, selfish, calculated reasons were proposed until one observer said simply, "Maybe she is just taking her marriage vows seriously, the part about 'for better or for worse.' " Imagine that, a prominent political figure who keeps her promises.

Thornton Wilder is best known as the author of the heart-warming play *Our Town* and the novel about why good people die young, *The Bridge of San Luis Rey*. He also wrote a quirky play, not often produced, called *The Skin of Our Teeth*. At the end of the play, the heroine says to her husband: "I married you because you gave me a promise. That promise made up for your faults. And the promise I gave you made up for mine. Two imperfect people got married and it was the promise that made the marriage. . . . And when our children were growing up, it wasn't a house that protected them and it wasn't our love that protected them. It was that promise."

Moses, at the moment of the Exodus, knew he had to make an important decision. No longer merely an advocate of liberation, he was now the leader of a newly emancipated people. His first acts in that capacity would set the tone for what image of themselves that band of former slaves would carry with them. Would it be an image of the pursuit of personal gain, of every man for himself? Or would his pledge to Joseph, an ancestor who had been dead for years, be their priority? His decision: I will set the example for my people that we will be a people who keep their promises.

The prophet Hosea spoke to the Israelites of a God whose love for them was so fierce that He could forgive their straying after strange gods and strange ways, a claim perhaps born out of the prophet's own experience of loving and forgiving an unfaithful wife. In words that a traditional Jewish man recites every morning at prayer as he binds the leather straps of *tefillin* around his fingers where one might wear a wedding band, Hosea said in God's name, "I will betroth you unto Me for all time; I will betroth you unto Me with righteousness and justice; I will betroth you unto Me with faithfulness and you shall truly know the Lord." What does it mean for God to betroth someone with faithfulness? I understand those words to mean that God's "wedding gift" to His people as they renew their covenant with each other will be the capacity for being faithful. God's gift to those whom He would love and call His own even though they have broken promises and not lived up to what they said they would do will be the capacity to be faithful, the strength to keep their word. God's loving gift to us to confirm our commitment to each other, to make sure that the covenant endures, will be the gift of enough strength to resist temptation, to choose integrity over self-interest even as Moses did on the eve of the Exodus.

The expectation that people will keep their promises, that husbands and wives will be faithful to each other, that business-men and -women will deliver what they committed themselves to deliver and customers will pay them for it as they promised to, that politicians will strive to be the same people in office that they represented themselves as being when they ran for office, is the glue that holds a society together. Should that glue weaken too much, should we ever begin to fear that no one can be trusted and that we are being taken advantage of because of our honesty, our society will fall apart. The benefit we gain from breaking a promise is all too clear and it is not surprising that many people are tempted by it. The cost of breaking a promise is harder to see—the loss of other people's trust, the loss of one's own sense of integrity, losing the security of living among people we can count on. As Moses understood, something inside us breaks—something that sustains our world breaks—when we break a promise, and something vital and indispensable is preserved when we are strong enough and good enough to keep our word.

6

It's Not All About You

"Now Moses was a humble man, more so than any other man on earth" (Numbers 12:3). How was it possible that Moses, the man to whom God spoke face-to-face, the man who called plagues down on Egypt, commanded the sea to split, and told the Israelites how to regulate every aspect of their lives, could have been more humble than the most anonymous farmer or slave?

The answer lies in a proper understanding of the commonly misunderstood word *humility*, which has taken on some unattractive connotations. As explanatory synonyms for the word *humble*, the dictionary offers such words as *meek*, *deferential*, and *submissive*, none of which would seem to apply to Moses. Readers of Dickens will hear the word *humble* and think of the smarmy, treacherous Uriah Heep, who was always boasting of his humility. (Isn't there something self-contradictory about *boasting* of one's humility?)

Humility can also connote false humility, a posture used to hide a large ego. The story is told that during Sigmund Freud's first visit to America, he was introduced to a prominent leader of the American Jewish community. They got to talking about who were the greatest Jews in the world. The community leader insisted that Freud would be high on that list. Freud asked him if he would include his own name on the list. The man shook his head vigorously and said, "Oh no, no, no. Certainly not me. Not at all." Freud commented with a smile, "One no would have been sufficient."

But there is a healthier way of understanding the term *humility*, one that connotes neither self-effacement nor false modesty. Humility is the realization that not everything that happens in life is all about you. Things may work out well, but you may not have been the primary reason for their success. Things may fail, but the failure may not have been your fault. If it rains on the day of your daughter's wedding or on every day of your beach vacation, that is just weather, and farmers and gardeners may in fact be grateful for it. It was not some cosmic conspiracy to deprive you of happiness.

Humility means recognizing that you are not God and it is not your job or responsibility to run the world. Some people are disappointed to learn that; most mentally healthy people are immensely relieved. Moses was able to surmount the problems and frustrations in his life because he understood that he was not God and could not be expected to be, and that God's plan for humanity did not depend solely on him.

The central prayer of the Jewish High Holy Day liturgy, the emotional high point of a long and solemn service, describes God opening the book of deeds for each of us, and examining the record of how each of us has lived in the past year. It then goes on to proclaim that "it is decided on Rosh HaShanah [New Year's Day] and confirmed on Yom Kippur, who shall live and who shall die, who shall flourish and who shall perish, who shall die by drowning and who by fire. . . ." That prayer always bothered me. We give it prominence in the service. It evokes the strongest emotional response of the entire day, and there is something profoundly moving about joining with a thousand voices to chant it together. But I don't believe it. I know that it is meant to be poetry, and one does violence to the meaning of a poem by taking it literally. I know the prayer doesn't really want us to believe that God actually has a dossier on me and on everyone else, recording each time I shaded the truth or pretended not to see a beggar on the street. I don't believe it is decided in September or October whether I and my congregants will make it through the coming year. If I believed that, there would be no point to my watching my diet, buckling my seat belt, or obeying traffic signals.

When I was caught in the San Francisco earthquake in 1989, barely a week after Yom Kippur, I never believed that I escaped harm because a few days earlier God had determined that I should have another year of life and condemned other people to die by fire. The prayer caused me a great deal of theological and intellectual discomfort until I came up with an acceptable way to understand it.

I now see the opening paragraph of the prayer, the part in which we are told that the book is opened and the entries are in our own handwriting, as a poetic way of saying that some of the things that will happen to me in the year ahead will be the result of things I do and choices I make. I deserve the credit and the blame for perhaps half the things that happen to me. If I eat and drink too much and never exercise, I have only myself to blame for any health problems that may ensue. If I put a favorite bowl too close to the edge of the table, I should blame myself, not gravity, if it falls and breaks. By the same token, if I am charitable, if I work at being a good husband and father and a good friend, then I can justifiably take credit for the good things those traits may lead to.

Then the second half of the prayer, the part about my fate being decided on Yom Kippur by forces beyond my control, is a poetic way of saying that many of the things that will shape my fate in the new year will be out of my hands, the result of biology, luck, and other people's choices. A driver can be involved in an automobile accident because he was careless, or he can be in an accident because even though he did nothing wrong, someone else was careless. Sometimes a business flourishes because the man at the top is good at what he does or it fails because of bad judgment on his part. But sometimes external events or market forces determine the good or bad result. Sometimes I get sick because I didn't take care of myself, sometimes because, even though I did everything right, I inherited some vulnerability from my parents or lived where the air and water were bad. Once I came to understand the prayer that way, I was able to accept responsibility for some things in my life while recognizing that many other things were due to events beyond my control.

That was how Moses was able to remain humble, and how his humility helped him cope with the frustrations and dead-ends of trying to lead an uncooperative nation. He understood that his successes were not his but God's, that he was only God's instrument, and that failures like the episode of the Golden Calf or the grumbling about the lack of food and water were arguments between the people and God, not between the people and Moses. That perspective kept him from becoming too proud when things went well and from feeling like a failure when they went badly.

Why is it so hard for us to accept the idea that it's not all about us, that we may not be responsible for all the good and bad moments in our lives? A newborn infant in its first months of life has not yet learned to distinguish itself from the world around it. It believes it is the world and the world is it. After a few months, when the infant has come to recognize that there is a world outside itself, it comes to see itself as the center of that world and the cause of all that happens. The child wakes up from a nap and all he has to do is cry to summon people to fuss over him. He is hungry; another cry brings someone to feed him. When he is wet and uncomfortable, someone changes him. The world seems to exist for no purpose other than to meet his needs. In the normal course of events, the child will reluctantly learn to leave that notion behind. He will learn to share his toys, to wait for meals, to get to places on time even if it means turning off the television in the middle of his favorite program. He will exchange the fantasy of omnipotence for the satisfaction of sharing life amicably with others.

But some people never learn that lesson, and most of us never learn it entirely. Bits of that infantile outlook remain hidden in our souls and emerge from time to time. Parents get grumpy for all sorts of reasons, from marital discord to the home team losing a football game, and children assume that they did something wrong to make the parent angry. By now, we know that when informing children about a marital separation the parents' first words should be, "This is not about you or anything you did," because children are quick to assume that whatever happens, for good or ill, is their doing.

Some people go through life believing it's all about them, expecting others to meet their needs with no thought of reciprocity. They become teenagers who manipulate friends for their own emotional, sexual, or financial benefit. They become bosses who make endless demands on their employees, from setting unrealistic performance goals to asking them to run demeaning personal errands. They become terrible husbands or wives who insist on winning every argument and having every disagreement resolved in their favor. They may feel like gods, but in truth their behavior is that of an infant.

In other, less extreme cases, the childish fantasy of grandiosity, being at the center of everything that happens, manifests itself in our tendency to feel guilty, to feel personally responsible every time something we were involved in doesn't work out as we had hoped. We are so guilt-prone, unable to accept the fact that there may be lots of reasons for something not working out, because at some perverse level, it feels good to feel bad. To assume the blame is to make ourselves feel important, indispensable. "The person died because I had angry thoughts about him." "My son was rejected by his first-choice college because I didn't improve his application essay enough." To be culpable is to be powerful, to be the one on whom everyone and everything depends, and although that sense of overwhelming responsibility can be exhausting (how does God manage to run the whole world without getting tired?), for a certain kind of person, there is something satisfying about it.

A man in my congregation sat in my office one evening and lamented the fact that his daughter was leaving her husband. Over and over, he cried, "What did I do wrong? Why is she doing this to me? How can I get her to see things my way?" I told him, "She's not doing it to you. She is choosing to do this with her life. It's about her and her husband, and you're at best a minor character in the drama. It may be a right choice, it may be a wrong choice, but it's a choice *she* is making, and if she feels she has to do it, I wish you could be supportive of her." But he wouldn't listen. To him, it was not his daughter's story. It had to be his story, the story of how she rejected his advice and broke his heart.

I had breakfast one morning with a man who had spent much of his adult life in prison, finally straightened out, and was now running a halfway house for released prisoners, to integrate them back into law-abiding society. I asked him, "Why did you do the things you did, knowing that you would almost certainly get caught, go to prison, and shame your family?" He answered with the self-awareness of a man who had found the courage to look at himself without illusions. "When something is missing inside you, there is something exhilarating about deciding that you're above the law, that the rules don't apply to you." That would explain the teenager who shoplifts even though she could afford to pay for the item six times over. It would explain the multimillionaire executive who breaks the law to gain, or keep from losing, what would be for him a trivial sum of money. Grandiosity, the opposite of humility, tells you that you are special, that the rules and prohibitions apply to other people but not to you.

Humility is the cure for these faults, the way to rise above them by lowering ourselves. The essence of humility is found in the advice, "Leave a little bit to God." Not everything in life is or should be up to you to do. A child's coming to terms with the fact that he is not the center of the universe and that he is not going to get everything he wants or even everything he deserves is sometimes spoken of as "the loss of innocence," the reluctant acknowledgment that life is unfair. To paraphrase something my teacher Mordecai Kaplan used to say, expecting the world to treat you fairly because you are an honest person is like expecting the bull not to charge you because you are a vegetarian. I like to think of it not as a loss of innocence but as the beginning of wisdom, the understanding that life may not be fair but it is not without all sorts of possibilities and compensations.

When something bad happens to us, we feel singled out by fate. We are convinced that everyone else out there is happy and healthy and only we are suffering. I have known people who took pleasure in being sick or suffering bereavement because it brought them the sympathy and attention they craved. In a perverse way, it validated their need to feel special, and in their minds elevated them above all those other people whose lives were lacking in drama. I have known others who went to great lengths to explain to me why their illness or their loss was worse than that of someone else in similar circumstances. (Anything is better than being ordinary.) Gregg Easterbrook writes in his book *The Progress Paradox:* "If you wanted something and didn't get it, clearance is given you to feel sorry for yourself. . . . When you're feeling sorry for yourself, you [are not going] to help others or show them kindness because you have a grievance against the world." But the response of humility would lead one not to think, My misfortune makes me more pitiable than anyone else on earth, but, My misfortune gives me a sense of kinship with other suffering souls out there.

When our son was ill and when he died, my wife and I felt that we were the only afflicted parents in a world of normal families. But as people came forward to comfort us, we realized how many people had that experience in common with us. My wife and I would hardly think of ourselves as being like the Rockefellers, the Kennedys, or the Bushes, but in fact they and we have known the pain of losing a child. That is why, when someone comes to see me in emotional pain, diagnosed with a serious illness, or grieving the loss of someone close, the best advice I can give that person is to urge him to join a support group. Find the company of others who are going through the same thing you are. In a support group, you learn that you are not alone. Similar things happen to all sorts of people. Your pain and your guilt are normal, typical responses. In a support group, people know how to comfort you, and you come to feel empowered when you realize that you know how to comfort them.

Once we understand, in all humility, that not everything that happens is about us or because of us, then personal sorrow need not, and should not, teach us to feel sorry for ourselves. It can and should teach us to feel solidarity with others. Adolescents, despite their tendency to self-centeredness, can be capable of stunning gestures of idealism and generosity when they let their own yearnings and disappointments teach them to understand the anguish of others rather than brood about themselves. Therapist Miriam Greenspan writes in her book *Healing Through the Dark Emotions,* "What connects us to others and to the world [is what] breaks our hearts." I don't think she is saying that compassion, opening ourselves to the pain of others, breaks our hearts. If that were the case, we would make every effort to avoid feeling another's anguish out of concern for our own well-being. I think she is saying that we can respond to the personal experience of heartbreak, as we will almost surely encounter it, in one of two ways. We can let our pain monopolize our thoughts to the exclusion of other people and their problems. Or we can let our own experience pierce the tough outer layer of our hearts and open us to compassion, becoming more complete human beings in the process.

Dr. Greenspan writes: "We all have stories about our suffering. Most of them are narcissistic stories, narratives in which the self is the exclusive focus. . . . Making the connection between our personal pain and the pain of the world gets us out of the isolation that the dark emotions tend to impose." She goes on to say that when people in mourning ask, "How dare the world go on turning, how can the sun shine as usual after what happened to me?" the answer is, "The world turns as it does precisely because [your] ego is not at the center of it." Best-selling author Karen Armstrong writes in her memoir *The Spiral Staircase:* "Compassion has been advocated by all the great faiths because it has been found to be the safest and surest means of attaining enlightenment. It dethrones the ego from the center of our lives and puts others there, breaking down the carapace that holds us back from the experience of the sacred." In other words, when humility leads us to see our pain and misfortune not as something that separates us from a world of lucky people but as something that connects us to a world of suffering people, it hurts less. Self-pity separates us from other people, leading us to resent them and leading them to resent us for focusing so narrowly on ourselves. With a modicum of humility, compassion, even holiness, can replace self-centeredness.

There is a part of us, the part that didn't entirely grow up, that would like to believe that the rules don't apply to us. Sickness and sadness can happen to others, but we deserve better because we are good people, because we are smart, honest, charitable, and religious. Other people have their share of tragedy and misfortune, but we will be spared. Other people get into automobile accidents or are diagnosed with cancer but not us. Then, when reality intrudes, we lose that sense of being different from everyone else but in its place gain an understanding of how much we really have in common with everyone else. Learning that we are not that different from others gives us the opportunity to learn from them how to deal with illness and disappointment.

Psychiatrist Irvin Yalom writes of a patient, an elderly widow, who could not get over her husband's death. She wept and grieved and refused to be comforted. Dr. Yalom, as her therapist, was unable to understand why. Then one day she was mugged and her purse with three hundred dollars in it was stolen. Remarkably and unpredictably, that troubling incident helped her come to terms with the loss of her husband. As Dr. Yalom understood it, she had led a relatively charmed life for most of her years—healthy, happily married, financially secure. That was why her husband's death was so "unacceptable" to her. Things like that only happened to other, more ordinary people. The mugging finally robbed her not only of her cash but of her illusion that she was immune to misfortune and that bad things would happen only to others. It forced her to realize that she was more like everyone else than she wanted to believe. As Mariana Caplan writes of her own experience of misfortune, "I lost my conviction that I could control my life."

But then, would we really want to be in control of life? Caplan goes on to muse, "If life obeyed our plans and expectations, then life would only be as wide as our undeveloped intelligence."

Some things that happen to people are authentically tragic—losing your life savings, losing a loved one, losing the physical ability to do something that is important to you. But most of the things that frustrate our hopes and derail our plans are aggravations when they happen but ultimately fall short of the level of tragedy. Very few arguments between husbands and wives are over matters important enough to be allowed to alter a relationship; most are just the result of pent-up annoyances, fatigue, minor resentments, or anger about something else entirely. Very few family conflicts rise to the level of *Hamlet*. Very few marital quarrels are as destructive as the ones in Edward Albee's play and movie *Who's Afraid of Virginia Woolf?*, in which two people really want to hurt each other mortally. Most quarrels turn out, in retrospect, to be thoughtless and exasperating but ultimately harmless and forgivable. When the writer Isaac Bashevis Singer lost many of his possessions in a fire, including the manuscripts of several stories he was preparing for publication, friends tried to console him in the wake of that tragic event. Singer told them, "No, it wasn't a tragedy. Nobody died. When a child dies, that is a tragedy. To lose things is an inconvenience."

This is where humility can save us from elevating the inevitable disappointments of life to the level of life-shattering tragedy. In act 4 of Shakespeare's *As You Like It*, the plaintive Orlando is professing his love for the elusive Rosalind, whom he hardly knows. He pleads for a kiss; she puts him off, saying, "I say I will not have you." Orlando responds that if she will not have him, "then in mine own person, I die" of unrequited love. Rosalind counters, "The poor world is almost six thousand years old, and in all this time there was not any man died in a love cause. . . . Men have died from time to time and worms have eaten them, but not for love." Her words would remind us that broken hearts, like broken legs, hurt but heal and that the scars they leave are testimony to our having had the courage to dream, to love, and to risk being hurt.

A woman who is feeling distraught and wondering how she can go on with her life because the love of her life has rejected her can make the mistake of saying to herself, Well, of course, I'm really not that attractive or interesting. Why wouldn't a desirable man reject me? A man fired from a job he had worked at faithfully for many years might say to himself, I probably deserved that. I guess I'm not as good an employee as I thought I was. Those responses might strike us as expressions of humility: Why did I ever think I deserved better? But true humility, grounded in a view of life that has taught us to keep in mind that we are not the only ones hurting, would have us think, All right, things like this happen. Smart people (my former beau, my former boss) make mistakes and someone just made a mistake by letting me go. Things like this have happened to lots of people and they got over it. I'll hurt but I'll get over it too. Life is a chain of good days and bad days. I've just had a bad day, so there ought to be good days ahead.

The hard way to learn that most of the disappointments in your life are relatively trivial, the hard way to learn the difference between tragedy and inconvenience, is to have something really serious happen to you. The difference will be unmistakable. I have sat with families from my congregation in the emergency room of a hospital while a loved one was being cared for and heard them say, "When something like this happens, I can't even remember what I was so worried about this morning." The easier, less painful way to learn that lesson is to learn it from other people's experience rather than our own. We all know people and have read about people who encountered misfortune and refused to let it define their lives, even as we know people who understood that lives of blessing and success were matters of good luck rather than anything they had earned. Moses, walking out of the palace and encountering a world of slaves and slavemasters, could have thought to himself, I am one of God's favorites and that is why my life is so fortunate and they are so miserable. A white man growing up in the racially segregated South or in a society in which women had no career options except to be teachers or secretaries, a person living in comfort in the United States while much of the world lives in squalor, might well have thought something similar: it is God's plan that I should be more fortunate than they. But Moses and many beneficiaries of accidents of birth rejected that view and thought to themselves, I was lucky; let me share my luck with the less fortunate. Moses "went out among his brethren," and brave men and women since the time of Moses have fought to distribute God's blessings more equitably among God's children.

This then is the meaning of humility: When something bad happens to you, you will get over it. When something good happens to you, it too may pass. You may or may not deserve it. You may or may not have earned it. It doesn't matter. Be grateful for it. And always remember that misfortune should not set you apart from happy, healthy people. It should connect you to all the other hurting people, and that means pretty much everybody.

We lose something, something we never really had, when we give up the infantile fantasy that the world exists to meet our needs, but we gain something as well. There is something liberating about the insight that we may be unique but we are not indispensable. Would we really want to be indispensable? Would we enjoy never being free to take a vacation, never allowed to make a mistake? Maybe the only truly indispensable people are mothers in the first months of a child's life, something many women find deeply fulfilling but a role they will outgrow soon enough. There are some people whose mistakes and failures can truly be disastrous—surgeons, judges, heads of state, generals of armies. I have seen side-by-side photographs of presidents of the United States taken on the day they were inaugurated and on the day they left office four or eight years later. They aged more than the passage of those years should have aged a man. The constant pressure, the genuine indispensability, the awareness of the consequences of a mistake wear a person down. Moses by contrast is described in the Bible as just as vigorous at the end of his life as he was when God first summoned him (Deuteronomy 34:7) despite the challenges and disappointments he encountered in leading a resistant people. His secret was humility. He realized that he was not God. He was one of God's many servants. If he could not do everything God wanted done, the rest would be done by another of God's servants at another time and place. That realization may be hard for our ego to accept, but ultimately it will be better for our soul.

7

The Mistakes
Good People Make

I am truly a lone traveler, and have never belonged to
my country, my home, my friends or even my immediate family with my whole heart.

Albert Einstein

W E STUDY the lives of great people to learn from them
what made them great and the ways in which we can
follow their examples. We study the lives of bad people in biographies and in fiction to try to understand what drives people to
be bad, why the inhibitions that keep us from acting out our
anger, our greed, our selfishness don't inhibit them and to reassure ourselves that we are not like them. But no human being is
perfect. The best of people will make mistakes, and by studying
where they went wrong, perhaps we can learn to avoid some of
the mistakes that even the best people make.

We have learned over the years that there are several components of the fully lived life. When Freud was asked what a

person needed to do to be happy, he answered in three words, "love and work." Today we can identify five strands of the good life.

A person needs a small group of other people to whom he is intimately connected, people to whom he matters a great deal and who matter equally to him. For most of us, we will find that in our families. For some—for example, celibate priests, single adults, widows and widowers, people estranged from their families—it will mean a small circle of very close friends.

Beyond that, we need a wider network of friendships and social acquaintances. The more people we know, the more our souls are nourished by those relationships. A friend of mine whose business consisted of selling advertising novelties, items like ballpoint pens with a company's name on them, realized one day that he did 90 percent of his business by phone or mail. He tried to save money by closing his office and working out of his home. A month later, he was back in the office. It turned out that he missed the camaraderie of the lobby coffee shop and the familiar faces in the elevator more than he could have anticipated. He became active in our town's Rotary Club, and I suspect that part of the attraction was having a group of friends to meet with for lunch once a week. Similarly, the experience of watching an athletic event, live or on television, is enhanced when it is shared with friends.

We need to be grounded in a faith. It may or may not be a "brand name" religion, but it should give us a way of making sense of the world and our place in it, helping us to understand the bad things that happen to us without our giving in to despair, and having reason to believe that tomorrow can be better than today.

Then, as Freud told us, we need to work. Paid or unpaid, we

need something that calls on our abilities and lets us feel competent. I have known too many people who looked forward to retirement so eagerly, only to find their lives lacking savor when they no longer had anything challenging with which to fill their hours. My father continued to go to his office every day until he developed health problems, when he was past eighty, not because he needed the money but because he needed to feel useful.

And finally, we need to feel that we are contributing to our world, paying the tax on the space we occupy and the air we breathe by doing something to make our world a better place, whether through our job, our church or synagogue, the local PTA, a civic organization, or our favorite charity.

Five elements of the complete life: family, friends, faith, work, and the satisfaction of making a difference. Most of us will agree on the need for all of them. Our biggest problem will be finding time in a twenty-four-hour day to do all five well. Too often, the problem will be which one gets first call on our time and energy, and which ones fall to the bottom of the list and are too often ignored.

Moses scored well on four of the five. He was certainly grounded in his faith. More than most men, he had a job that challenged him and the satisfaction of knowing that what he did changed people's lives for the better. He had a large network of people with whom he interacted regularly. For Moses, as for so many successful men, if there was to be a soft spot in his life, if anything was to be shortchanged, it was most likely to be his family.

The Bible doesn't tell us very much about Moses' family life. We read about his sister's watching over him when he was an infant. We know that his older brother, Aaron, served alongside him as high priest. We know that he married and had two sons. But to learn how he got along with his wife, his children, and his siblings, we have to read between the lines of the biblical narrative, and what we find there is evidence of the kind of mistakes that even very good people make.

Chapters 18–20 of the book of Exodus describe how the Israelites, having just fled Egypt and crossed the Red Sea, come to Mount Sinai for their encounter with God and the revelation of the Covenant. But before God speaks to the assembled throng, we read:

> Jethro priest of Midian, Moses' father-in-law, heard all that God had done for Moses and for Israel His people, how the Lord had brought Israel out of Egypt. So Jethro, Moses' father-in-law, took Zipporah, Moses' wife, after she had been sent home, and her two sons, one of whom was named Gershom . . . and the other Eliezer. . . . Jethro, Moses' father-in-law, brought Moses' sons and wife to him in the wilderness where he was encamped at the mountain of God. He sent word to Moses, "I, your father-in-law Jethro, am coming to you with your wife and your two sons." Moses went out to meet his father-in-law; he bowed low and kissed him. Each asked after each other's welfare, and they went into the tent. Moses then recounted to his father-in-law everything that the Lord had done to Pharaoh and to the Egyptians for Israel's sake. . . . (Exodus 18:1–8)

You probably noticed that the Bible refers to Jethro as Moses' father-in-law six times. Twice it emphasizes that he is coming to restore Moses' wife and children to him, so that they can be a normal family. He even introduces himself to Moses that way, saying, "I, your father-in-law Jethro, am coming to you with your wife and your two sons." We then read how Moses greets Jethro, brings him into his tent, and tells him all that has happened to him since he left Midian to return to Egypt. *But we never read of Moses greeting his wife and children.* Despite the repetition of the term *father-in-law,* Moses seems to greet Jethro as a visiting dignitary, not as a member of the family. Maybe Moses had a private, intimate reunion with his wife and children that the Bible never tells us about. But I find it equally likely that Moses was so absorbed in preparing for the revelation at Sinai that he had no time for them. Have the pressures of leadership so totally consumed Moses, so totally taken over his personality, that he has no soul left for his wife and sons? Has so much happened to him that Zipporah and his sons seem to belong to another self, someone he used to be before he left to become God's emissary?

I have seen families hurt by similar mistakes. How often have we seen men achieve success and prominence in business or politics and decide that the wife of their youth, the hometown girl they married after college, was no longer a suitable accoutrement for their new station in life? (Think of Reese Witherspoon's boorish beau in *Legally Blonde* dumping her with the line, "If I'm going to be a senator, I need a wife who is more Jackie and less Marilyn.") Could it be that every time Moses looked at Zipporah, it reminded him of a chapter in his life he was less than proud of, the years he spent as an anonymous, penniless fugitive in Midian after killing an Egyptian?

Even more common is the ambitious young man who leaves his family emotionally without even realizing that he has done it. Many years ago, I wrote an article for one of the women's magazines entitled "I Hate to Admit It, But My Wife

Was Right." (To my chagrin, they changed the title to "Make Time for Family"!) I confessed that the one thing in my life that I wished I could go back and do differently was my excessive devotion to my career in my thirties when our children were young. My wife and children needed me at home, but I was so intent on being the best rabbi anyone had ever seen, so intent on making a name for myself, that my family got only my left-over time. By the same token, I have known some women who, when they had a baby, withdrew the concern and affection they had previously shared with their husband and focused it all on the child.

When the Bible (Numbers 12:1–2) describes Miriam and Aaron speaking against Moses "because of the Ethiopian woman he married" (the reference must be to Zipporah; we know nothing of Moses taking a second wife), a tradition in the commentaries understands that to mean that they spoke out *on behalf of* their sister-in-law, Moses' wife. The commentators surmise that Moses had been neglecting his wife, spurning opportunities for intimacy lest God suddenly summon him. In biblical law, a man or woman who comes in contact with menstrual blood or seminal issue is ritually impure and must immerse in a ritual bath later that day. This is not because the Bible considers sex to be dirty or defiling. On the contrary, it is because people regarded those bodily fluids that have the power to generate life with such awe and reverence that anyone who had contact with them would be "radioactive" for hours. When Miriam, sympathizing with her sister-in-law, says, "Has the Lord spoken only through Moses? Has He not spoken through us as well?" she is saying that she and Aaron also periodically receive the word of God but that has not prevented them from maintaining a life of marital intimacy with their mates. She is warning Moses not to let his role as a prophet, important as it surely is, absorb his entire identity as a person. He has to remember to be a husband and father as well.

We don't really know what ever became of Moses' children. Hardly anything is ever heard of them. There is an obscure, uncorroborated, and possibly unreliable reference in I Chronicles 26:24–26 to the effect that the grandson and great-grandsons of Moses served as keepers of the treasury in Solomon's Temple three hundred years after the time of Moses. (That must have been one elderly grandson.)

That nothing is known of Moses' descendants is not unusual. It is all too common for the children of great men to grow up to be very ordinary despite that genetic inheritance or to have serious problems living up to the famous name they inherited. Sometimes the father casts so large a shadow that he makes it hard for his children to find the sunshine they need to grow and flourish. Sometimes the father's achievements are so intimidating that the child just gives up any hope of equaling him. But mostly, I suspect, it takes so much of a man's time and energy to be a great man—great in some ways if not in all ways—that he has too little left to be a father. Nelson Mandela's daughter is quoted as saying to him, "You are the father of all our people but you never had the time to be a father to me." Eleanor Roosevelt once shared the rueful insight that "a man in high public office is neither husband nor father nor friend in the commonly accepted meaning of those words." Albert Einstein's son Hans, who went on to have a distinguished career as a scientist, commented sadly, "The only project my father ever gave up on was me."

(And yet we must ask: Would the world be as well off without the epochal insights of Einstein, the leadership of Franklin

Roosevelt, and the heroic contributions of Mandela? Could they have been better husbands and fathers and still have done the things they did? I would like to believe that God did not give us a world in which doing great things publicly required major sacrifices at home. I would like to believe that it was the personality of an Einstein or a Roosevelt, not the demands of their careers, that shaped both their successes and their failures, and that the theory of relativity could have been discovered and the Second World War won by men, or women, who found time for their families, indeed who were nourished by the support of their families.)

Some years ago I read an article in a magazine circulated to clergy. It was a fictional account of a pastor in a medium-sized church who had a dream one night in which a voice said to him, There are fifty teenagers in your church. You have the ability to lead forty-nine of them to God and lose out on only one. Inspired by the dream, the pastor threw himself into youth work with imagination and energy. He taught extra classes for the adolescents in his community. He raised funds to take them on class trips. And it worked. He won a national reputation in his denomination for his work with young people. And then, one night, he discovered that his sixteen-year-old son had been arrested for dealing drugs. The boy had turned bitterly against the church and its teachings, resenting his father for having had time for every sixteen-year-old in town except him, and the father had never noticed. His son was the fiftieth teenager, the one who got away.

We know almost nothing about what happened to Moses' children while Moses was teaching other people's children to honor their parents. But there is at least a hint that there may have been problems. There is a strange story in the Bible of how the tribe of Dan, vulnerable to Philistine attacks after the death of their hero and fellow tribesman Samson, migrated to the north of Israel, conquered a town on the Lebanese border, and made their home there, a safe distance from the Philistine threat. Along the way, they were joined by a priest of the tribe of Levi who had sculpted an idol and led services worshipping it. We read that when they reached their new home in the north, "the Danites set up the sculpted image for themselves, and Jonathan the son of Gershom and the grandson of Menasseh, and his descendants, served as priests to the tribe of Dan until the land went into exile" (Judges 18:30). This would seem to be an unremarkable story, telling us that somewhere in the extreme north of Israel, as far from its religious and cultural center as one could get, a renegade tribe and a renegade priest worshipped an idol, something expressly forbidden by the Covenant, except for one detail that should attract our attention. At several points, the Bible lists the descendants of Menasseh, one of Jacob's twelve sons. He never had a son named Gershom. Moreover, the sons of Menasseh were not Levites; the Levites were a separate tribe. But we do know someone who had a son named Gershom: Moses! (See Exodus 2:22, among other citations.) Furthermore, Moses was a Levite, and in Hebrew there is a difference of only one letter between the spelling of Moses' name and that of Menasseh. The conclusion seems inescapable that Moses' grandson had strayed so far from what his grandfather devoted his life to teaching that he and his descendants earned their living leading worship of idols at an illegitimate shrine. Only the delicacy of an editor, changing one letter in an obscure narrative, tried to hide that embarrassing fact. We don't know anything else about this Jonathan son of Gershom, but I have known a lot of people like him, young men and women who could find no outlet for their anger at their families except to do the one thing that they knew would hurt their family the most.

THE SUMMONS to be a prophet and a spokesman for God may also have complicated Moses' relationship with his older brother, Aaron. At the outset, their relationship seems ideal, free of jealousy, free of conflict, with a clear and mutually agreeable division of labor. When Moses protests that he is "slow of speech and slow of tongue," God tells him, "There is your brother Aaron the Levite. I know he speaks readily. Even now he is setting out to meet you and he will be happy to see you" (Exodus 4:14). At the time of the Ten Plagues, when Moses is reluctant to afflict the Nile River because it had saved his life when he was an infant, it is Aaron who turns the waters of the Nile to blood. But later things seem to change.

I had a congregant who taught anthropology at a nearby university. He once showed me a paper he had written titled "The Authoritarian Triad." Its thesis was that if there are two leaders in a community, one of whom has a positive relationship to the people being led, constantly praising and affirming them, while the other has a negative relationship, scolding and expressing dissatisfaction, there will be a negative relationship between the two leaders. It is almost like an electrical connection, where a positive charge and a negative charge require another negative charge to keep them in balance. Imagine a family in which the mother is strict and rigid and the father is permissive and easygoing. Isn't it likely that there will be conflict between the two parents? Picture a church or synagogue with a senior pastor who over the years has grown relaxed and accommodating about some rules, making his peace with the low level of seriousness on the part of the congregants. Then a young assistant comes in, fresh out of seminary, with a zealot's determination to see that things are done as they should be. How will they get along? (The good cop–bad cop routine we may be familiar with from television crime shows does not contradict this. Both detectives have a negative relationship to the suspect, but one pretends to be friendly.)

Might something like that have happened to Moses and Aaron? Might Aaron, the firstborn, have resented the prominence of his younger brother? Moses was the prophet, bringing God's law and God's demands down from the mountaintop. Aaron was the high priest, officiating at God's altar when people brought their animal offerings of celebration or atonement. I can picture Aaron complaining, Why do you get to give all those speeches telling people how to live and what behavior God approves of, and I get to clean up the entrails of dead animals? What kind of shared leadership is that? And I can imagine Moses responding, Yes, I give speeches about how to live, but do you ever listen to what I have to say? I'm always telling people not to do things they are eager to do: Don't eat that, don't earn your money that way, keep your hands off your neighbor's wife. And all the while, you're telling people who have broken those rules, It's all right, we can work something out. Jewish tradition pictures Moses with a perpetual frown and a stern, judgmental voice and pictures Aaron with a kind face and a soft voice. The Talmud at one point urges scholars to "be disciples of Aaron, loving peace and loving people as a way of bringing them closer to the Torah."

When I described the episode of the Golden Calf in chapter 2, I omitted several crucial details concerning Aaron's role in what happened. When the people became restless in Moses' absence, they "gathered against Aaron and said to him, Make us a god who will go before us for that man Moses who brought us out of Egypt, we do not know what happened to him" (Exodus 32:1). Aaron, perhaps as a delaying tactic to stall until Moses returns, perhaps out of an inability to stand up to people and say no to them, tells them to collect all of their gold and jewels, which he then takes and fashions into a statue of a calf. After Moses comes down from the mountain, breaks the tablets, destroys the calf, and punishes the ringleaders, he asks Aaron, "What have you done?" Aaron gives the pathetic, almost comical answer: "The people were unruly and bent on evil, so I took all their gold and jewelry and threw it into the fire, and out came this calf" (Exodus 32:24).

I picture Moses saying to his brother, How could you do this to me? I turn my back on you for a few days and you ruin what took me years to bring about. And I imagine Aaron responding, You weren't there. You don't know what it was like. You went off to your mountaintop for six weeks and left me alone with this rebellious mob. I was just trying to distract them so they wouldn't burn down the whole camp, and this is the appreciation I get.

If Moses was the prophet, uttering commandments from the mountaintop, proclaiming "Thou shalt not!" insisting on high standards as the demanding voice of God the Father, and if Aaron was the priest, meeting people where they were, accepting them in all of their imperfection, expressing the forgiving smile of God the Mother, that would explain why, when Moses died, we are told "the Israelites mourned him . . . for thirty days." (Deuteronomy 34:8), but when Aaron died, we read "*all* the house of Israel mourned Aaron for thirty days" (Numbers

20:29). Moses was revered, Aaron was loved, and it would be understandable if each envied what the other had and he lacked.

There may have been another factor contributing to tension between Moses and his older brother. When we read at the end of the book of Exodus that Moses is instructed to "anoint [Aaron's] sons as you anointed their father, that they may serve Me as priests" (Exodus 40:15), we understand that to mean that Moses is to use the same ritual to consecrate this second generation of priests to God's service that he employed to consecrate Aaron the first time around. But one commentator finds a deeper message in those words. When Moses anointed Aaron as the first high priest in Israel's history, he had no reason to be jealous. After all, his role was a good deal more prominent than Aaron's. But when he was called on to anoint Aaron's sons to succeed their father, he might well have had cause to envy Aaron, realizing that he would never see his own sons succeed him. God thus commands him, "Anoint the sons *exactly as you anointed their father*" (my italics), just as wholeheartedly and without jealousy or resentment. That will be the hallmark of true love and friendship, the ability to take pleasure in another person's happiness. It takes a special kind of love to celebrate someone else's financial success or the birth of his or her child when you suspect it will never happen to you. It takes a greatness of soul for a childless woman to be happy for her sister's or sister-in-law's pregnancy and to listen without bitterness to her complaints of morning sickness. It is a sign of true friendship to be able to wholeheartedly congratulate a good friend and coworker who gets the promotion that you were hoping for. When Freud writes that every man is jealous of another man's success and the sages of the Talmud write that every man is jealous of another's success except a father of his child and a teacher of his student, I would like to believe that the rabbis are right and Freud was wrong, but experience tells me I can't be certain of that.

If there was a modicum of jealousy in Moses' seeing Aaron's sons following in their father's path, that would shed light on a strange and troubling biblical incident. It tells of the day the Tabernacle was to be dedicated to house the Ark of the Covenant and to symbolize God's presence among the people. Aaron in his role as high priest was to officiate at the consecration of the Tabernacle, the culmination of months of work, dressed in his finest robes and attended by his four sons. It should have been his proudest day. But we read that two of Aaron's sons, Nadab and Abihu, "offered a strange fire before the Lord, one He had not commanded. Fire came forth from the Lord and consumed them both and they died" (Leviticus 10:1–2). We are troubled by the tragic death of two young priests, struck down as they served God in His holy tabernacle. We are puzzled by the reference to the "strange fire," whatever that may refer to. But as much as anything else, as we read the story we have difficulty understanding Moses' response to what happened. His first words to Aaron, "This is what the Lord meant when He said, I expect holiness from those closest to Me" (Leviticus 10:3), seem surprisingly cold and unlikely to comfort his brother. Perhaps Moses' own experience had taught him that one sometimes pays a price with one's family for total dedication to a cause. He may have been saying, I sacrificed family in God's service; why shouldn't you have to? Or perhaps he was saying, At least your sons were close to God when they died, as if a bereaved father would find comfort in that.

A few moments later, he scolds Aaron and his remaining sons for letting that incident interrupt the ceremony, telling them that they should have completed the offering of purification as the ceremony called for and only then gone off to grieve privately. Aaron has to remind his brother that it is improper for a priest in mourning to participate in the sacred offerings (Leviticus 10:16–19).

That exchange prompts one of the classic commentators to write: "See what anger can do to a wise person's mind. Even Moses, when he was angry, forgot the law [about priests in mourning]." When I read that comment years ago, I assumed that Moses was angry at the tragedy that had befallen his nephews on what should have been a day of celebration, so upset that he could not think straight and forgot the relevant laws. I thought he may even have been angry at God for letting it happen. Now I suspect there was something more at work. Might it be that Moses could not properly comfort his brother because he was jealous of him for having such a perfect family, for having sons who would share his role and follow in his footsteps, for having the time to be a devoted husband and father because his job did not absorb all of his time and energy? Did Moses speak and act so shockingly inappropriately because he at some level felt guilty for wishing that something like this would happen to Aaron, and doubly guilty when it actually did happen? Psychologists use the German word *schadenfreude* to refer to the guilty pleasure people often feel in contemplating another person's misfortune. Is it possible that even the satisfaction of being Moses, the man who brought God into people's lives and changed the world, was not enough to protect him from being jealous of someone who had something he did not have—the affection of a wife, the loyalty of children, the undiluted love of the people he served?

In my book *How Good Do We Have to Be?*, I noted that the first time the word *sin* appears in the Bible, it is not connected with Adam and Eve and the incident in the Garden of Eden. The first mention of sin is in the story of Cain and Abel (Genesis 4:7), and it is not a reference to Cain murdering Abel but to his being jealous of Abel. For me, that is the original sin, to overlook the blessings you have and to be consumed with envy because someone else has something that you don't.

IF THESE family problems and estrangements could happen to a great man like Moses, if they could happen to an Einstein, to a Mandela, how can we guard against their happening to us? The first thing we can do is to think seriously about our priorities, where to allocate our time and our emotions, and then act on those conclusions instead of letting events and other people's demands make the determination for us. If we can't have everything on our wish list (and few people can), what things are we prepared to sacrifice so that we can have the others?

The movie *A League of Their Own* is about women's professional baseball during the Second World War, when most of the male athletes were in the military. At the end of the movie, Geena Davis, who is the most talented player in the league, deliberately drops the ball in the last inning of the last game of the World Series, losing the game but enabling her less talented sister, a player on the opposing team, to be the heroine instead. The boost in confidence that would give her troubled, insecure sister means more to her than winning a championship. I suspect a lot of men walked out of the theater after the movie shaking their heads and thinking to themselves, What a dumb movie. How can you be a professional athlete and deliberately lose an important game because you don't want to make the players on the other team feel bad? Can you imagine the Yankees getting together and saying, Why don't we let the Red Sox win this year? We've won so often, and it would mean so much to them. And I imagine a lot of women walked out thinking to themselves, Wasn't that touching? What a sensitive thing to do. What's the big deal about winning? So this year you win, and next year somebody else wins, and three years from now you're a question in Trivial Pursuit and nobody remembers who won three years ago, but in the meantime you've broken the heart of someone you claim to care about.

If we are to be truly wise, if we are to realize the fullness of our humanity, we need to understand the rightness of both attitudes. We need the masculine drive of wanting to do our best and the feminine insight that part of being our best has to include sensitivity to the feelings of people we are dealing with, especially the people closest to us. (Had Geena Davis's sister suspected that Davis had deliberately dropped the ball to let her win, she would have been deeply hurt and offended. The effort would have done more harm than good. Children and adults alike are not well served by being given things they know they have not earned at the hands of well-meaning others who don't trust them to achieve those things themselves.)

The second thing we can do to avoid the trap into which even great men have fallen is to be very clear in our own mind that *we are not defined solely by our work*. I don't know if other societies do what we do here in the United States, answering the question "What do you do?" exclusively in terms of what

we do for a living (putting some women in the awkward position of saying, "I don't do anything; I stay home and raise the
children," as if molding the soul of a child were less important
than going to an office). Other societies have more holidays,
more vacation days than we do (here, the higher one rises on
the ladder of business responsibility, the more likely one is to
work on those days). Few people in other cultures, given a
shorter workweek, use that free time as many Americans do, to
take a second job.

In the question-and-answer period following one of my lectures, I was once asked, Would you rather be Moses or Einstein? My immediate response was, "Given that both of them
are dead, I don't see that it makes much of a difference." I then
went on to say that given the tendency of most people to over-
value what they personally find hard and underappreciate what
comes easily to them, which is why couch potatoes are more
impressed by athletic skill than other athletes are, and given
that understanding theology always came fairly easily to me
but physics, math, and science baffled me, I think I would have
appreciated being Einstein, able to look at the universe, see
relationships no one had seen before, and translate those relationships into mathematical formulas.

Less than an hour later, I realized that I had given the wrong
answer. Both men were blessed by God with the ability to see
and understand things beyond the ken of ordinary people.
Each changed the way we understand the world. Each had his
flaws. But Einstein taught us to understand the world of things,
the conflicting pulls of momentum and gravity, the hidden
energy locked inside an atom. Moses taught us to understand
the world of the human spirit, the conflicting pulls of selfishness and generosity and the potential energy hidden in every

human soul. It should have been clear to me that understanding the mysteries of human behavior is infinitely more important than understanding the relationship of matter to energy. We may *work* with things, with computers or legal briefs or inventories, but we *live* ever so much more intimately with people. The biographer Doris Kearns Goodwin, who knew Lyndon Johnson well, wrote of him in her book *Lyndon Johnson and the American Dream,* "He surmised perhaps he would have been better off spending more time with his children and grandchildren, leaving a different, perhaps more personally fulfilling legacy." She goes on to quote Erik Erikson: "The richest lives attain an inner balance comprised of work, play and love in equal order. To pursue one at the expense of the others is to open oneself to sadness in older age."

Did Einstein come to understand that lesson, after years of abusing his first wife and neglecting his children even as he changed the way we understand the universe? Does my congregant understand it when he spends three nights a week on the road away from his family in order to provide them with an upper-middle-class lifestyle? Should a researcher close to discovering a vaccine for AIDS stay late at her laboratory to reach her goal sooner, or should she make sure she leaves early enough to give her young children supper and put them to bed? And did Moses realize, when he took up the challenge of being God's messenger, what price his wife and children would have to pay for his greatness?

It is probably unrealistic to expect perfection, not from Moses, not from Einstein, not from ourselves. It is probably too much to expect ourselves or anyone to be equally competent in all five dimensions of the complete life. But as a friend of mine likes to say, "You can have it all, just not all at the same time."

Maybe we can adjust our priorities as our life situation changes, emphasizing what is important at one stage of our lives and deferring the emphasis on other aspects of life for a later date. I have known many families who had no time for worship or serious study when their children were young but made it central to their lives when their children were grown and they were facing the transition into middle age. I have known many people who worked hard at their jobs for many years and then became active in their communities or in charitable causes to fill the void of an "empty nest" or to provide the sense of validation they no longer found in the workplace. Moses did so many things right that thousands of years later we still benefit from them. But perhaps we can learn from the one thing he did least well. We can learn to avoid the mistake that even good people will too often make, neglecting the basic needs of our souls and asking our families to sacrifice their own well-being while we set off to change the world.

8

How to Write Yourself a Happy Ending

THERE remains one more lesson to be learned from the life of Moses, and to learn it we will need to make sense of one of the most puzzling incidents in Moses' life. The incident occurs in the fortieth and final year of Israel's wanderings, a year that will see them come to the border of the Promised Land. Chapter 20 of the book of Numbers begins by telling us of the death of Miriam, Moses' older sister. We can only speculate as to what her death meant to Moses. She was the first of his siblings to die. She had been more than a sister to him, virtually a surrogate mother, watching over him as an infant. We can see her as a trusted adviser, a calming, reassuring influence in his life. And now she was gone. Her death, and Aaron's death at the end of the chapter, may have moved Moses to wonder how much longer he had to live, how much more time he had to accomplish what remained to be done.

Miriam has died, and we read that the people have no water

to drink. There is an intriguing connection between Miriam and water. Even her name carries connotations of water; the Hebrew word for water is *mayim,* and the word for sea is *yam.* She first appears by the banks of the Nile watching over her baby brother. She leads the Israelites in a song of celebration after the crossing of the Red Sea. A rabbinic legend tells of a miraculous well that would appear in the desert wherever Miriam pitched her tent. And now she was dead and the people were desperately thirsty.

The people come to Moses and Aaron with their complaints, wishing they had remained in Egypt where at least there was food to eat and water to drink, wishing they had died earlier in the desert and been spared this anguish. God tells Moses and Aaron to assemble the people in front of a large rock and to order the rock to produce water. Moses says to the assembled throng, "Listen, you rebels, shall we get water for you out of this rock?" (Numbers 20:10). He then strikes the rock twice with his rod (instead of commanding it verbally) and water pours forth for the people and their flocks.

God is displeased with Moses and says, "Because you did not trust Me enough to affirm My sanctity in the sight of the Israelite people, therefore you shall not lead this congregation into the land that I will be giving them" (Numbers 20:12). Moses will not be permitted to accompany the Israelites into the Promised Land. His forty years of wandering, like his forty days on the mountaintop, will end in frustration rather than fulfillment.

It is hard not to be shocked and dismayed at the harshness and seeming arbitrariness of the punishment. Some traditional commentators, eager to justify God at Moses' expense, fasten on his saying "Shall *we* get water for you?" (emphasis by the commentator), taking credit for the miracle himself instead of giving glory to God. Some modern commentators fault Moses for using a tactic that had worked in a previous generation, striking the rock to bring forth water (Exodus 17:1–6), and assuming it would be equally effective a generation later. One even suggests that it was an act of kindness on God's part to bar Moses from the Promised Land. For years he had dreamed of it as a perfect place, the perfect setting for a people to devote themselves totally to the service of God. Were he to enter the real land, he would inevitably be disappointed. The reality could never match the land that existed in his imagination. That is an experience many of us will recognize, the dream vacation that turned out to be disappointingly ordinary, the "perfect" date who turned out to be a self-involved bore, the job that had been our lifelong dream that, when we finally attained it, is anything but what we thought it would be. The dream is a source of hope, of motivation; the reality will all too often be a letdown. God, the writer suggests, did Moses a favor by shielding him from that disillusionment.

For many years, I found the key to understanding the passage in Moses' addressing the angry mob as "you rebels." It said to me that he was burned out, worn down after years of trying to lead a stiff-necked people. His followers were in many cases two generations younger than he was. They had grown up in a different world than he had. For them, Egypt was history rather than biography. Perhaps Moses could not relate to them and in his frustration dismisses them, as many older people dismiss younger ones, as "rebels." When he strikes the rock, I can imagine that what he really wanted to do was strike some of the complainers with his rod, and was taking his anger out on the rock. At that point, God realizes that Moses' years of leadership are coming to an end. He is too tired, too angry, too sensitive to criticism to be an effective leader. When God tells him that he will not lead the people into the Promised Land, it is not so much a punishment for disobeying God as the recognition that Moses had been the right leader to bring a nation of slaves out of Egypt and lead them to Sinai, but he would be the wrong leader to take them into the battle for the Promised Land. He was too old, too tied to the way things had been done in the past. God was saying to Moses as He had once bid Moses say to Pharaoh, "It is time to let My people go."

I now find myself having second thoughts about that interpretation, after reading a psychologically oriented biography of Moses that suggests another way of understanding the story. The author, Dr. Dorothy Zeligs, points out that Moses often refers to *God* as a rock: "Give glory to God, the Rock whose deeds are perfect" (Deuteronomy 32:3–4). "Jeshurun . . . forswore the God who made him and spurned the Rock of his support" (Deuteronomy 32:15). She suggests that when Moses hits the rock instead of speaking to it, it is not the people with whom he is angry. It is not the people on whom he is taking out his frustration. He is angry at God, the God who imposed this impossible burden on him, the God whose demands separated him from his brother and deprived him of a normal family life. When God rebukes Moses, saying, "Because you did not believe in Me to sanctify Me in the sight of the people," He is saying, Moses, you let your problems with Me, your anger at Me, prevent Me from working the miracle I had in mind, a gentler, more impressive miracle than what you ended up with. When Moses complains to the people three times in the opening chapters of his final oration that "God was angry at me because of you" (Deuteronomy 1:37, 3:26, 4:21), was he projecting his own feelings onto God? Did he really mean to say, *I was angry at God* because of you, and that is why I will never get to enter the Promised Land?

Being angry at God can be a good thing. I often urge congregants who have suffered a grievous loss or been diagnosed with a life-altering illness to express their anger at God over what has happened to them, assuring them, "The God I believe in is not so fragile that your anger will hurt Him nor is He so petty that He will strike you a second time for speaking up to Him." There is a classic Yiddish short story, "Bontshe the Silent," about a man who has had a miserable, tragic life but never complains, deeming it a form of piety to refrain from challenging the way God sees fit to run His world. Some people reading the story see Bontshe as a paragon of religious faith, but I follow the view of most critics that the author is showing us a man who has lost an essential part of his humanity, the capacity to rail against life's unfairness having been beaten out of him. I believe that God wants us to get angry at all the suffering and unfairness that clouds His world. I believe it is the highest form of piety to be outraged by the crimes, natural disasters, accidents, and illnesses that befall good people, even as I believe God is outraged by them. And I believe that it is less harmful to vent that anger on God than to be angry at your doctor for not being able to cure you, your parents for having made mistakes raising you, or your mate for not knowing the words or deeds that would make you feel better.

But our anger at God should be like other episodes of anger we may direct at people around us. We should vent our feelings, get them out of our system, and then get over them, valuing the long-term relationship more than the temporary falling-out. If the anger is still there after several days, I begin to suspect that someone may have reasons for keeping it on life support and not letting it die a natural death. Too many people refuse to get over their anger, sometimes because remaining angry is their way of insisting that they were right and the other party was wrong, sometimes because the only power they feel they have over the one who hurt them is their refusal to get over being angry. But in almost every case, nursing the grudge does more harm to the person holding it than it does to the target of the anger. It has been compared to swallowing poison in order to make someone else sick.

I have known too many people who could not enjoy the last third of their lives because the first two-thirds did not turn out they way they had hoped, and they were angry at God for that. Their last years, sometimes last decades, were marked by unhappiness and resentment because they never made it to the "promised land." Their careers, their marriages, their families never quite turned out as they hoped. These people never got over their anger at God for the way their lives turned out, for all the things that happened or didn't happen in their lives. Often these were people who might have had much to look back on with pride and pleasure, but they could never see things that way. They were not only alienated from the church or synagogue, they were alienated from life itself, in the way that self-pity and constant complaining about things that happened years ago can drive others away and leave you lonely, giving you one more thing to complain about.

Somehow Moses was able to reconcile himself with the God who had demanded so much of him and taken so much from him. How did he do it? How does a person get over that bitterness, that sense of having been cheated by life? The answer, I believe, involves a delicate balance of remembering and forgetting.

It is interesting to note that, in the last few years, there have been a number of movies dealing with the theme of people losing their memory. Some are comedies, with people not recognizing lovers or family members, to the consternation of those unrecognized. Some are dramas; a man who "knows too much" has his memory erased by evil scientists. To me, the most intriguing was a movie titled *Eternal Sunshine of the Spotless Mind*. It tells the story of a young couple who meet and fall passionately in love, and whose relationship ends in bitterness and anger. They find the memories of what they shared so unbearably painful in the light of their breakup that they choose to go through an experimental medical procedure to erase their memories of each other from their minds, leaving them with neither the glow of having known love nor the pain of its loss. First the young woman, then the man, visit a psychiatrist who has learned how to identify the precise location in the brain of a specific memory and how to erase it. Twice the movie quotes the philosopher Nietzsche: "Blessed are the forgetful for they get the better even of their blunders," that is, it is a blessing to be able to forget the mistakes in our lives rather than live with the painful memories. (The young woman's name is Clementine, hinting that her fate is to be "lost and gone forever.")

I think stories about people losing their memory appeal to many moviegoers because they are walking around with painful memories that make it hard for them to enjoy today and contemplate tomorrow with hope. They wish there were some way of washing their minds clear of those memories. For some, the memories are personal ones—failed relationships, jobs terminated, having been the victim of crime or betrayal. For others, the memories are global: thoughts of war, genocide, earthquakes, floods, or other mass disasters. Many Americans are still traumatized by the events of September 11, 2001, when we not only lost three thousand innocent victims of terrorism but lost our sense of invulnerability as well, and we have never been the same since. I remember seeing a cartoon shortly after that day, showing a woman saying to her travel agent, "Where do I want to travel to? I'd like to go back to September 10." It is no wonder that the prospect of erasing painful memories appeals to us. (The human mind may already have a built-in mechanism for doing that. A friend of mine was brutally attacked in a hotel parking lot one night many years ago. All he remembers is getting out of his car, and waking up several hours later in a hospital.)

But if we could, would we really want to erase those memories? At the climactic moment of *Eternal Sunshine*, a memory is triggered in the young man's brain, in order to be erased. It is the memory of a time when he and his lover were together and he says to her, "This is the happiest I have ever been in my life." At that point, he wonders why he is having the happiest moment of his entire life erased from memory just because its aftermath is so unbearably painful.

In the spring of 1995, I was invited to Oklahoma City to meet with families who had lost loved ones in the bombing of the Murrah Federal Building, and to conduct a workshop for clergy and social workers who would be trying to help those families heal. Ten years later, I was invited back to introduce a "Week of Hope" to mark the tenth anniversary of the bombing. At a public gathering of several thousand people, I raised the questions, "Would we be better off if we could forget that terrible day, if the media didn't remind us of it, if we hadn't turned the site of the destroyed building into a museum and memorial park? Would Americans be better off if no television station ever again showed the scene of an airplane flying into the World Trade Center? Or are we better off holding on to those memories of what happened and who we lost, bitter and painful as those memories might be?" The answer I suggested was, first, that we probably cannot forget, even if we wanted to, even if we decided like the young people in the movie that we would be better off without the memories. The people we loved and lost, the dreams we dreamed and lost, are woven too deeply into the fabric of our identity ever to be extracted. And second, even if we could somehow forget, we owe it to ourselves and to those we lost to remember.

I told the audience that evening, "There are ghosts walking the streets of Oklahoma City this week. Listen to those ghosts; hear what they are saying. They are saying, Remember us, because the only place we still live is in your memories. Remember us, because our lives, whether they lasted long or were cut short, were filled with love, with plans made and hopes shared, and those moments of love and yearning deserve to be remembered. Let them be our legacy to you."

Naomi Shemer was a successful and much-loved composer of popular songs in Israel. More than an entertainer, she had the ability to capture her people's hopes and dreams in her songs, to the point where it is hard to think of Israeli society without them. (We might compare her to Irving Berlin in the United States writing "God Bless America" and "White Christmas.") In 1967, on the eve of the Six-Day War, she wrote a ballad, "Jerusalem of Gold," expressing her longing for the Old City of Jerusalem and the site of Solomon's Temple. When, a month later, the war ended with Israel in control of Old Jerusalem, the song became the unofficial anthem of the city. Some six years later, Shemer wrote another widely beloved song, "The Honey and the Sting." It takes its title from an incident in the Talmud about a man who sticks his hand into a bee-hive looking for honey, is stung, and walks away muttering, "I can do without the honey and without the bee sting." Shemer, in her song, takes the opposite approach. Her position is, I want the honey and I accept the sting that often comes with it. I want to know the pleasures of love, loving a husband, loving a child, even if along with those pleasures comes the vulnerability to losing the one I love. I want to yearn for achievement, for fulfillment and recognition, even though I understand that many people want those things and few people attain them.

If we could not temporarily put out of our minds some of the painful moments of our past, how would we find the courage to go on? How would we steel ourselves to get on airplanes, let alone risk loving again, if we were obsessed by thoughts of how things sometimes turn out badly? But if we could not remember, would we still be us? Those painful moments are such a large part of making us who we are, as the young man in the movie ultimately realizes. I met a man once who was a social worker in Miami Beach, dealing largely with elderly Jewish survivors of the Nazi Holocaust. Ostensibly his job was to keep them informed about changes in Medicare and Social Security. But he told me that whenever the group met, all they wanted to talk about were their experiences in the death camps. He once asked one of them, "Those must have been incredibly painful times. Why do you hold on to the memories so tenaciously?" The man answered, "You're right, they were very bad times, worse than anything you could imagine. But what happened there is such an important part of who I am. Without those memories, am I still me or am I someone else, someone more fortunate?"

Of all the ailments that people fear as they grow older, the scariest is being afflicted with Alzheimer's disease. Cancer, congestive heart failure, and Parkinson's disease are terrible and little by little rob of us our capacity to enjoy life. But should we find ourselves diagnosed with one of them, we can fight them. We can do the things we love to do while we still have the ability. We can say the things that we need to say to our loved ones while we still can. We can cooperate with our doctors. But with Alzheimer's, once it takes over our brains and destroys our memories, we cannot fight off the gathering darkness. In a sense, we are no longer ourselves.

My mentor, Rabbi Mordecai Waxman, one of the three teachers to whom I have dedicated this book, when he had to officiate at a particularly sad funeral, would often include in his eulogy the Greek tale of the waters of Lethe. The legend tells that when a person dies, he or she comes to the river that is the boundary between the land of the living and the land of the no-longer-living. The boatman whose task it is to ferry disembodied souls across the river would tell the new arrivals that they were entitled to drink of the waters of Lethe, the waters of forgetfulness, before they crossed over. If they drank, they would forget everything that had happened to them on earth. They would forget the painful moments but also the pleasant moments. They would forget the pain of illness and rejection, but also the joys of health and love. It would be as if they had never tasted life. If they chose not to drink, they would be left with those memories for eternity. According to the tale, almost no one, no matter how bitter their days had been, chose to drink the waters of Lethe.

Some years ago, a friend of mine wrote a memoir about her husband's lingering death as a result of Lou Gehrig's disease, and of her subsequent battle with depression. She asked me to write the foreword to the book. My foreword began with the words "Life can be painful if you do it right." To wish to forget the hope because it wasn't realized, to try to cleanse your mind of the beautiful dream because it didn't come true, is to miss out on life altogether, because life is designed to be lived in an alternation of hours of sunlight and hours of darkness. I have been in Alaska and in northern Europe on days when the sun barely rose over the horizon. Nurses in Anchorage told me how, in the winter months, they brace themselves for increases in alcoholism, depression, and abuse of women and children. Something unhealthy happens to people who have to live in near-total darkness, deprived of sunlight, even as the author of the Twenty-third Psalm looks to God to lead him through the valley of the shadow so that he would not have to dwell permanently in the darkness. At the other extreme, I have been in Patagonia, at the southern tip of South America, with nothing but water between me and Antarctica, on days when the sun set so late that I had no patience to stay up until it got dark and many of the locals tried to function on three hours of sleep. I could not live very long in either climate. My life needs a reasonable balance of light and darkness.

Several decades ago, the psychiatrist Dr. George Vaillant embarked on an ambitious long-term study of young men from different backgrounds. He hoped to identify traits of men in their teens and twenties that would predict successful careers and home lives when they were in their forties and contented old age when they were older. The culminating volume of his research, *Aging Well,* appeared a few years ago. Vaillant was pleased to learn that for many people, old age did not have to be a time of loss, regret, and "playing out the string." Just as the last innings of a baseball game are often more exciting than the earlier ones, just as more typically happens in the last twenty minutes of a movie than in the first twenty, just as many a good book comes together and begins to "make sense" in the last few chapters, a person's last years, if done right, can be, in Browning's phrase, "the best of life for which the first was made."

Vaillant identified two traits as keys to contentment late in life. One is having a growing circle of friendships, what Erikson called "a widening social radius," instead of a shrinking number of people in one's life. He would urge us to make a deliberate effort to cultivate new friendships as old friends move out of our lives due to death or relocation. We should go so far as to take a personal social inventory of our lives every six to twelve months, asking ourselves, Have I made a new friend recently? The second key is nurturing our ability to forgive slights and injuries. When you find yourself spending as much or more time looking back at your past as you do contemplating your future, make the effort to look back with gratitude more than with regret, with fondness more than with bitterness. Gregg Easterbrook, in *The Progress Paradox,* makes a similar point, writing that "people are happy if they are optimistic, grateful and forgiving. . . . If you think only about your disappointments and unsatisfied wants, you may be prone to unhappiness. If you're aware of your disappointments but at the same time thankful for the good," contentment comes more easily. In Vaillant's words, "people who make lemonade out of lemons fare better [in old age] than people who turn molehills into mountains." As Thomas Moore puts it in *The Soul's Religion*, "I have made many mistakes and done a lot of foolish things, and when I look back at the person I was, I feel affection for him."

Moses spent the last half of his life in the company of people who made demands of him and complained about everything to him. Yet he flourished, reaching old age with "his eyes undimmed and his vigor unabated" (Deuteronomy 34:7). How did he do it? Perhaps when people came to him with demands, instead of thinking to himself, Why are they bothering me? he said to himself, These people need me. They depend on me. I am not a superfluous old man; I am an important contributor to their lives. When they complained, he might have thought to himself, They have come to me to share with me their dreams of how life could be better.

Vaillant found that people who were unhappy in their late years were suffering not from a lack of material things but from a lack of love, companionship, and optimism. In one of his key findings, he writes, "It is not the bad things that happened to us that doom us, but the good people who happened to us at any age that facilitate an enjoyable old age."

I ONCE had to speak at a memorial service for a teenage girl who had been abducted from her job as a lifeguard and murdered. Despite intense search efforts, her body was not found until three years later. Speaking to her stricken family and her grieving, angry high school classmates, I said: "How can we leave this service and go on living in a world where things like this can happen? Look at it this way: One person did a vicious, destructive thing. Dozens of people, friends, neighbors, and total strangers contributed their time to the search effort, trudging through woods and fields in rain and mud. Hundreds of people offered their prayers and sent letters of encouragement. One man devoted to evil; five hundred men, women, and young people devoted to helping. I can live in a world like that."

Often in my congregational years I have officiated at the funeral of an elderly man or woman, only to be called on to do the same for the surviving spouse six to ten months later. The death certificate may have listed cancer or heart disease as the cause of death, but I often suspected that the real cause of death was loneliness and self-pity, the sense of having nothing to live for and no one to share life with, the inability of the surviving spouse to fill the empty space with new friends and new interests.

Vaillant's second commandment for writing a happy ending to your biography is the willingness to forgive. Forgiveness is not a matter of exonerating people who have hurt you. They may not deserve exoneration. Forgiveness means cleansing your soul of the bitterness of "what might have been," "what should have been," and "what didn't have to happen." Someone has defined forgiveness as "giving up all hope of having had a better past." What's past is past and there is little to be gained by dwelling on it. There are perhaps no sadder people than the men and women who have a grievance against the world because of something that happened years ago and have let that memory sour their view of life ever since. They resent young people for their liveliness and the possibilities still open to them. They assume, usually wrongly, that everyone is out to cheat them. Life has disappointed them and they spend their last years complaining about it.

Moses had his reasons for being angry at God, and he may have revealed his anger when he struck the rock. He must have remembered times when the Israelites took their unhappiness out on him, blaming him for the heat, the food, the uncertainty of their wandering, maybe even blaming him for the laws forbidding theft and adultery, not to mention gossip, and rarely crediting him with having led them out of slavery. He likely remembered nights when his wife had become a stranger to him because of his preoccupation with God's word and God's work. He may have resented that God's demands created a barrier between him and his children and grandchildren, leaving him and his brother each jealous and resentful of the other. He may have felt cheated out of so much a person might have looked forward to in life. But he got over it. He kept his memories, the dreams he had had for himself, for his family, and for his people, even as he kept the broken fragments of the original Ten Commandments. They spoke to him of what it felt like to dream, what it felt like to yearn, not only what it felt like to fail.

I read recently of a young artist who thought he was on the way to the fulfillment of his ambition when a major gallery arranged an exhibit of his work. He was thrilled by the response of gallerygoers on his opening night, but woke up the next morning to the shattering news that his exhibit had been vandalized overnight. Canvases had been slashed, a bronze sculpture stolen, and a ceramic pot on which he had spent hours of creative love smashed to pieces. He was understandably distraught, unable to understand why some people are driven to destroy things, especially things that are beautiful. He felt that it was his life, not only his artwork, that had been vandalized. Had he turned to me in his grief and pain, I might have told him how Moses gathered up the broken pieces of what had until then been his glorious dream, the fragments of the original Ten Commandments, and carried them with him through all the years of wandering in a desert. He did this not to relive the pain and disappointment, not to tear open a scab that covered his emotional wound so that it would never heal. He held on to those broken pieces of stone to remind himself that he once dreamed a beautiful dream, and that dream shaped and defined him and continued to shape and define him even after he realized it would not come true in the way he had dreamed it. I would have urged the young artist to take home the fragments of his clay pot and cherish them, not to remind himself of the world's cruelty (why should the malice of one sick, destructive person outweigh the praise and admiration of dozens?) but to remind him of how he sought to create beauty and how he had succeeded in doing that.

Therapist Estelle Frankel writes in her book *Sacred Therapy* of how she used the story of Moses and the shattered tablets to heal a patient who had trouble accepting the world's imperfections and its unreadiness to support her dreams. The woman felt like a failure and was angry at the world for the way her life had turned out. As the client approached her fortieth birthday, Dr. Frankel devised a ritual for her to symbolize her freeing herself from the conviction that the world should be fair and people should get what they deserved, in short, to free herself from "the tyranny of the dream." The woman wrote down all of her childhood hopes and dreams of how she imagined her life would unroll, dreams of a fulfilling marriage and exemplary family, dreams of professional success and recognition. She then placed that document in a beautiful ceramic vase that she owned and cherished. Then, in the presence of her therapist, she smashed the vase and burned the paper. In Dr. Frankel's words, "smashing the vase, something she had been deeply attached to for a long time, became a powerful symbol of letting go of the past and allowing life to bring change. In grieving over her lost hopes and dreams, [the client] began to feel more ready to accept her real, though imperfect life."

And then, in imitation of Moses, the woman took the broken pieces of that cherished vase home and made them into a mosaic (interesting word!) to serve as a perpetual reminder of how she had once hoped and dreamed, how she had been disappointed, and how she had overcome disappointment, and was prepared to play the cards that life had dealt her instead of futilely wishing that life had turned out otherwise.

Joan Chittister, the former nun, writes in *Scarred by Struggle, Transformed by Hope*: "Surrender does not mean that I quit grieving what I do not have. It means that I surrender to new meanings and new circumstances. . . . I surrender to meanings I never cared to hear: She did not love me. They do not want me. What I want is not possible. . . . I surrender to the circumstances of life." She goes on to say: "Courage, character, self-reliance and faith are forged in the fire of affliction. We wish it were otherwise."

But it is rarely otherwise. The sad but inescapable truth is that very few people make it to the "promised land." Few people get everything they yearn for, and most of us don't get everything we deserve. I too wish it were otherwise. I wish there was a world I could move to where everyone who loved would be loved in return, where every kind person would be treated kindly by fate and by her neighbors, a world where all ailments could be cured by the weekend and all biopsies turned out to be benign. But I don't live in that world and neither does anyone else. Ask too little of life and you run the risk of coming to the end of your days never having tasted many of the pleasures God put on earth for you. Ask too much of life and you virtually guarantee heartbreak, disappointment, and the risk of thinking of yourself as a failure.

I think of Moses at the end of his life, this man who had climbed mountains to bring the word of God to mankind, climbing one last mountain for a glimpse of the land he would never set foot in. On that last day, was he remembering the triumphs, the Exodus, the sea divided, the establishing of the Covenant? Or was he remembering the complaints of an ungrateful nation, the loneliness that marked him as God's special agent? I would like to think that he remembered it all, and decided that the good days outnumbered the bad days, in significance if not in quantity. Perhaps he contemplated the fact that it is a quirk of human nature to feel pain more deeply than we feel joy, to take the good for granted and be outraged by the bad. I would like to think that Moses came to the end of his life prepared to forgive God for all the unfairness that exists in His world. I would like to think that he understood that a person will never achieve much in his life unless he aims high, and to aim high is virtually to assure oneself of a measure of failure.

Mariana Caplan writes at the end of her book *The Way of Failure,* "Are we going to use our remaining time to finally love well, to cherish others, to forgive them and to forgive ourselves?" Moses, at the end of his book, shows his greatness in the last moments of his life by singing a hymn of praise to God (Deuteronomy 32) and by blessing the people he had quarreled with for so long (Deuteronomy 33). A commentator imagines him saying, All my life I have scolded this people. Let me end my days by blessing them. His story is not a story of uninterrupted happiness (is anyone's?), but he *chooses* to give it a happy ending. Though it is not in his power to dictate the end of the story, it remains in his power to choose how he will respond to God's final decree. Given the opportunity to write the end of the story, Moses chooses to articulate pride rather than regret, gratitude rather than bitterness, praise rather than envy.

Archbishop Oscar Romero of El Salvador, shortly before he was assassinated in 1980, wrote: "We accomplish in our lifetime only a tiny fraction of the magnificent enterprise that is God's work. . . . We cannot do everything, and there is a sense of liberation in realizing that. This enables us to do something, and to do it very well. It may be incomplete, but it is a beginning." I would like to think that Moses realized that and found it comforting to know that he had done much and that God had other instruments to do what Moses had left undone.

I hope this book will help you to see your life that way, to think of love gained and love lost, of acceptance and rejection, of memories that continue to thrill and of memories that continue to hurt, of people who were close to you who are now distant and of people who traveled a distance, a spiritual as well as a geographical distance, to be close to you. If you succeeded at some things, you blessed the world by it. If you failed at some things, that was an inevitable part of being human, of your reach exceeding your grasp.

In the Grace After Meals in the Jewish tradition, we ask God to bless us "as You blessed our forefathers Abraham, Isaac, and Jacob, with a full and complete blessing." But the Bible tells us of how their lives were marked by fertility problems, quarrels with neighbors, conflicts between husbands and wives, between parents and children. What sort of blessings were those? I can only understand the phrase "a full and complete blessing" to mean the experience of life in its fullness, tasting everything that life has to offer, the bitter and the sweet, the honey and the bee stings, love and loss, joy and despair, hope and rejection. The blessing of completeness means a full life, not an easy life, a hard road, not a smooth one, a life that strikes the black keys and the white keys on the keyboard so that every available emotional tone is sounded.

If you have been brave enough to love, and sometimes you won and sometimes you lost; if you have cared enough to try, and sometimes it worked and sometimes it didn't; if you have been bold enough to dream and found yourself with some dreams that came true and a lot of broken pieces of dreams that didn't, that fell to earth and shattered, then you can look back from the mountaintop you now find yourself standing on, like Moses contemplating the tablets that would guide human behavior for millennia, resting in the Ark alongside the broken fragments of an earlier dream. And you, like Moses, can realize how full your life has been and how richly you are blessed.

Harold S. Kushner is Rabbi Laureate of Temple Israel in Natick, Massachusetts. He is the author of ten books, including *When Bad Things Happen to Good People, Living a Life That Matters,* and *The Lord Is My Shepherd.* In 1995, he was honored by the Christophers, a Roman Catholic organization, as one of fifty people who have made the world a better place in the last fifty years. In 1999, the national organization Religion in American Life honored him as clergyman of the year. He lives with his wife in Natick.

A NOTE ON THE TYPE

This book was set in Monotype Dante, a typeface designed by Giovanni Mardersteig (1892–1977). Conceived as a private type for the Officina Bodoni in Verona, Italy, Dante was originally cut only for hand composition by Charles Malin, the famous Parisian punch cutter, between 1946 and 1952. Its first use was in an edition of Boccaccio's *Trattatello in laude di Dante* that appeared in 1954. The Monotype Corporation's version of Dante followed in 1957. Although modeled on the Aldine type used for Pietro Cardinal Bembo's treatise *De Aetna* in 1495, Dante is a thoroughly modern interpretation of the venerable face.

Composed by Creative Graphics, Inc.,
Allentown, Pennsylvania
Printed and bound by R. R. Donnelley & Sons,
Harrisonburg, Virginia
Designed by Virginia Tan